|The American Puritans Series|

# The Mystery of Christ

THE
AMERICAN
PURITANS

# THE
# MYSTERY
## OF
# CHRIST

——INCREASE MATHER——

*Edited by P.J. Mills*

PETERBOROUGH

H&E
*Publishing*

*The Mystery of Christ*

Copyright 2021 by P.J. Mills

All rights reserved. No part of this edition may be reproduced in any form without the written permission from the author.

Published by: H&E Publishing, Peterborough, Ontario

This volume is a gently edited and modernized version of the 1686 first edition by Increase Mather (1639–1723) which is in the public domain: *The Mystery of Christ Opened and Applied. In Several Sermons Concerning the Person, Office, and Glory of Jesus Christ.* Printed at Boston in New-England, 1686.

Paperback ISBN: 978-1-989174-84-5
Ebook ISBN: 978-1-989174-85-2

"Yes, doubtless, and I count all things but loss, for the excellency of the Knowledge of Christ Jesus my Lord." Philippians 3:8

"And unto all the riches of the full assurance of understanding, to the acknowledgement of the Mystery of God, and of the Father and of Christ." Colossians 2:2

"These things have I written to you that believe on the name of the Son of God, that you may know that you have eternal life, and that you may believe on the name of the Son of God." 1 John 5:13

## Contents

The American Puritans Series ............ ix
Introduction ............ xi

### The Mystery of Christ

Preface ............ xix
Introduction from the Author ............ 1
1. Covenant of Redemption ............ 7
2. Jesus Christ Is the Son of God ............ 21
3. Jesus Christ Is Over All ............ 45
4. Jesus Christ Is Man as well as God ............ 59
5. Two Natures of Christ ............ 72
6. Jesus Christ Is the Mediator ............ 87
7. God the Father Is Fully Satisfied ............ 115
8. Human Nature of Christ ............ 131
Scripture Index ............ 153

# The American Puritans Series

Over the last fifty years there has been a renewed interest in the Puritans. In past generations, works by the English Divines sat dusty and derided, but soon found new life through the efforts of D. Martyn Lloyd-Jones, the Banner of Truth Trust, Reformation Heritage, and others. Today, many of the once-forgotten Puritans are household names in the Christian community—men like William Perkins (1558-1602), Richard Sibbes (1577-1635), Thomas Watson (c. 1620-1686), Samuel Rutherford (1600-1661), Richard Baxter (1615-1691), John Owen (1616-1683), John Bunyan (1628-1688), Matthew Henry (1662-1714), and others.

However, during the Great Migration (1630-1640), not a few Puritan leaders fled persecution and made their way across the Atlantic Ocean to settle in the American Colonies. These early American Christian leaders were not only pillars in the church, but also acted as spiritual and intellectual fathers of a great nation. But many of these faithful pastors are relatively unknown, their work is barely read, and their publications have long been out of print.

*The American Puritans Series* exists to reintroduce the work of these first Christian leaders to a modern audience.

Each reprint will consist of the author's original work, yet gently edited and modernized for the ease of the reader. By the grace of God, this series will help rekindle a love for the writings of the Puritans whose theology was built on the biblical doctrines of the Reformation. May a whole new generation see Christ afresh through the work of our spiritual ancestors.

Nate Pickowicz<br>
Series Editor

# Introduction

*P.J. Mills*

The Mather name is undoubtedly one of the most notorious names in the history of American Christianity. Sadly, the first thing that comes to the minds of many when hearing of the Mather family is not their voluminous contribution to American Puritanism, but rather the events which took place at the infamous Salem witch trials. However, most present-day Christians (and non-Christians alike) are simply unaware of the Mathers' role in the event; informed more by popular culture than historical witness.[1] As a result, the Mathers (and many of the New England Puritans for that matter) have been most unfairly dealt with over the last 300 years. I believe this is to the detriment both broadly to our country, and more specifically to the Church.

While it is important to keep in mind when reading these men that they were clay-footed sinners, there is much to be celebrated in the writings of the American Puritans, in particular, the Mathers. Quite frankly, some of their writings (and theology) were less than helpful. But I believe there are a plethora of

---

[1] Increase Mather wrote a book titled *Cases of Conscience Concerning Evil Spirits (1693)* wherein he denounced the means of evidence that were used to condemn the accused witches. This book was instrumental in changing public opinion on the trials and ultimately bringing them to a close in that same year.

books, articles, pamphlets, and sermons which will greatly edify the Church of our day. With this in mind, I am hopeful that more of the writings of these American giants of the faith will see the light of day as I believe they have much to offer us.

## Increase Mather: life & ministry

Increase Mather was the son of the Puritan minister Richard Mather who immigrated to Massachusetts in 1635 during the "Great Migration." Richard would faithfully serve as a pastor in Boston, Massachusetts until his death in 1669. Increase was born in 1639 as the youngest of six brothers. A bright intellect, he was admitted to Harvard at the age of 12, and he graduated with his bachelor's degree five years later at the age of 17. Mather immediately left the colonies following his time at Harvard to study at Trinity College in Dublin where he obtained his Master of Divinity two years later. Mather preached in England until the restoration of King Charles II in 1661. Just prior to the Act of Uniformity and the resulting "Great Ejection" of Puritan ministers from their pulpits, Mather returned to Massachusetts. Quite remarkably, Mather was called to be the pastor at the North Church in Boston and he would hold this pastorate until his death some 62 years later.[2] In addition to being a faithful preacher of the gospel, Increase Mather was a voluminous writer (though not nearly as voluminous as his eldest son Cotton who wrote over 450 books). In his lifetime he authored 130 books in total. He wrote on a broad range of subjects. These subjects included History: *A Brief History of the*

---

[2] Mather Increase, "Mather, Increase, 1639-1723. Papers of Increase Mather: An Inventory." Harvard University Archives, UAI 15.860, 24 Feb. 2005, Accessed on 19, Feb. 2019.

INTRODUCTION

*War with the Indians, and Early History of New England;* Providence: *Remarkable Providences, Ichabod, and The Voice of God in Stormy Winds;* Science and Astronomy: *Several Reasons Proving Inoculation is Lawful and Blessed by God,* and *A Discourse Concerning Comets,* Witchcraft: *Case of Consciences, and Wonders of the Invisible World,* and Christian Doctrine: *Practical Truths Plainly Delivered, A Guide to Christ,* and the present volume that you are holding in your hand, namely, *The Mystery of Christ, Opened and Applied.*

In 1685, Mather was appointed to be the president of Harvard. He was the first American born president of the university,[3] and he served as president of the university until 1701. Much of his tenure was mired in political controversy and he was largely ineffective in this leadership capacity. In 1688, Mather departed the colonies for England in an attempt to negotiate with the Crown to keep the colony's political charter. Here we see something of the citizen that Mather was. He was not only a brilliant intellect and a faithful pastor, but he was also a politician who served the cause of his native colony. Mather remained in England for four years but was unsuccessful in renewing the old charter. He did, however, successfully negotiate a new charter altogether which provided Massachusetts with more self-governance than any of the other colonies at that time.[4]

Mather's unwillingness to compromise on his social principles would ultimately lead to his political downfall as president of Harvard in 1701. However, the political failings of

---

[3] Mather. "Mather, Increase, 1639–1723. Papers of Increase Mather: An Inventory."

[4] Mather "Mather, Increase, 1639–1723. Papers of Increase Mather: An Inventory."

xiii

Mather would not ultimately define his life. Edmund Calamy, who wrote the preface to Mather's Memoirs, said the following of Mather: "Dr. Mather was vehemently set against all sin and impurity, and bent upon spreading practical Godliness, and promoting brotherly love, in the whole course of his ministry; and securing the peace and liberties of his native country, by his conduct, to the utmost extent of his influence."[5] While Mather was a staunchly convicted Puritan man, he was not a man who was uncharitable or unwilling to compromise on secondary issues. During Mather's four-year trip to England, he commonly visited religious dissenters of both Congregational and Presbyterian backgrounds, and was vocal about his desire to unite Congregational and Presbyterian churches.[6] He desired to see greater unity among Christ's people in his day. In these regards, he is an exemplary model of a pastor for us in our day.

**Death & legacy**

After resigning from Harvard, Mather withdrew from political life altogether and devoted himself solely to his pastorate and writing. He would continue preaching until 1722 when health issues prevented him from continuing. Mather died on August 23, 1723 at the ripe old age of 84. In the last year of his life he suffered from many illnesses and maladies which weakened him and prevented him from preaching. These illnesses did not

---

[5] Increase Mather, et al. "The Preface." *Memoirs: of the Late Reverend Increase Mather, D.D., Who Died August 23, 1723* (London: John Clark and Richard Hett, 1725), 14.

[6] Mather, Increase. "Mather, Increase, 1639–1723. Papers of Increase Mather: An Inventory." Harvard University Archives, UAI 15.860, 24 Feb. 2005, Accessed on 19, Feb. 2019.

## INTRODUCTION

seem to dampen his spirit though. Leading up to his death, he was often quoted as saying, "the infinite mercy of God, and the infinite merit in Christ, keep me above all discouragements."[7] In life and in death, Christ was supreme in the life of Increase Mather.

It should be noted by the reader that the American Puritans were not second-rate theologians. Most of them were every bit as brilliant, if not more so in some cases, than their English counterparts. Mather is no exception to this rule and he was held in high esteem by many of his peers. An example of this can be found in the works of that famous English Puritan John Flavel. In 1688, Flavel wrote an exposition of the Westminster Larger Catechism. This would be one of the final books that Flavel wrote in his lifetime and Increase Mather was asked to write the introduction for this work. Mather was viewed by some as the last true American Puritan and the final bastion of orthodoxy amid a quickly apostatizing New-England. In his preface to Mather's memoirs, Calamy places Mather shoulder to shoulder with the great Puritans and Reformers. He writes, "This Dr. Mather, to whose life I have been desired to prefix a preface, brings up the rear of them, as good old Dr. Gisbert Voetius did that of the members of the Synod of Dort, and Dr. Wallis, that of the divines who sat in the assembly at Westminster."[8] The reader of this work will notice Mather alluding to and quoting many well-known Puritans and Reformers such as Owen, Goodwin, Ursinus, Voetius, Vossius, and Grotius. Mather was well schooled in orthodox Puritan theology and

---

[7] Mather, Increase, *Memoirs: of the Late Reverend Increase Mather, D.D., Who Died August 23, 1723* (London: John Clark and Richard Hett, 1725), 98.

[8] Mather, *Memoirs*, 11.

*Mystery of Christ*

was a theological giant in his own time. It is a great tragedy that his works have been largely neglected in our present day. It is my hope to see much more of his work put into print in the coming days for the edification of Christ's Church.

**Editorial note**

This present work was written by Increase Mather in 1686. In Mather's words, it is a collection of sermons and sacramental meditations on the person, divinity, offices, and glory of Christ. This work was intended not primarily for the advanced theologian (though they may absolutely benefit from this work as well) but the layman who desires to know Christ more. As such, it is written in a very readable and devotional manner. This work has been gently edited and modernized. I have sought to retain the author's original style with some slight modifications. For example, he cited all of his Scriptures in italics but I have used modern convention and placed all citations in quotes. He likewise uses italics to emphasize key words and phrases and these have been, for the most part, left alone. I have modernized many archaic terms where I felt it was needed and left others (when useful) with a note on the definition of the word. Several Scripture references were misquoted in the original work so I have updated the references to ensure they are referring to the proper verses. Additionally, I have added in many footnotes on key doctrines, heresies, and theological terms for the general edification and knowledge of the reader.

You will notice that this work is arranged in the classical Puritan manner: the text is opened, the doctrine is examined, reasons are provided for the doctrine, applications or uses are given, and final exhortations are delivered. My hope and prayer is that you the reader are greatly edified by this Christ exalting

## INTRODUCTION

work, and if you are reading this and find yourself to be apart from Christ, that you would turn to Christ in faith and be saved. Mather states the following as his intention for writing this book, "I have not sought my own profit, but the profit of many that they might be saved. But in a more peculiar manner I have designed your edification. And I will confess to you, that no subjects ever insisted on by me, have had so much of my heart, as these which I now present unto you." I concur with Dr. Mather that there is no subject more important as that which is found before you in these pages— the person and work of Jesus Christ. I found this book to be doctrinally rich, soul stirring, and deeply devotional. This book will present you with rich doctrinal truth about Christ and His gospel and it will do so in a personal and approachable manner. In these dark and Christless days, I long to see reformation in the Church, true gospel revival, and the salvation of many souls. My heart's desire is that this work proves useful in the edification of Christ's Church and the salvation of souls. Christ is altogether lovely and there is truly no greater object of our affections or our attention. Mather exhorts the reader in this work saying, "he who grows in the knowledge of Christ, will grow in grace." I hope and pray that the information and important doctrines contained within these pages would not only lodge firmly in your head, but would also deeply affect your heart and stir up your affections for the Lord.

P. J. Mills<br>
May 6, 2019

# Preface

I am unfit and unworthy to pass any judgment upon these excellent sermons, which I have read over and over with much delight and satisfaction. I shall only say that they are in my opinion very much to the purpose, recommended to intelligent readers by their solidity and succinctness, comprising in a little room the choicest notions that refer to the subjects discoursed on: They are also well levelled to the meanest capacities, and thereby singularly fitted to the ends designed.

Urian Oakes[9]

---

[9] Urian Oakes was an English born minister and teacher. He was ejected from his ministry in 1662 due to the Act of Uniformity and eventually moved to New-England in 1671 to become a minister at the Church of Cambridge. Oakes became the president of Harvard University in 1675 and he held the position until his death in 1681.

# Introduction from the Author

To the Second Church and Congregation at Boston in New-England.

My Dearly Beloved,
   Our Lord in His last and most heavenly prayer for His disciples has said that "this is life eternal to know the only true God and Jesus Christ whom He has sent (John 17:3)." I have therefore, in the course of my ministry among you (you know) preached concerning Christ more than on any other subject. And I have singled out the few sermons emitted herewith, partly because the truths insisted on are of the highest importance; but also, in that they are much opposed by men of corrupt minds in this evil and adulterous generation. It was the dying complaint of a late worthy, "Never (says he) was there an age since the name of Christian was known upon the earth, wherein there was such a direct opposition made unto the person and glory of Christ, as that wherein we live. We have now a great number who oppose the person and glory of Christ under a pretense of sobriety of reason, as they vainly plead. Yes, the disbelief of the mysteries of the Trinity and the incarnation of the Son of God, the sole foundation of the Christian religion, is so diffused in the world, as that it has almost devoured the power and vitals of it. Of all the evils which I have seen in the

days of my pilgrimage now drawing to their close, there is none so grievous as the public contempt of the principal mysteries of the gospel."[10] Thus that excellent man! It is not impossible but you also, may be tried whether you will hold fast what you have received. I have therefore, thought it my duty to endeavor that you who are my flock, may have that by you, which will (by the help of Christ) be a means to settle and establish you in the present truth.

Moreover, I verily fear that many professors of religion are not so clear and well-grounded in these great principles of Christianity as ought to be. Some years ago, there was a man who came to me expressing his desires of satisfaction about a momentous truth of the gospel. He told me that he was not clear in his understanding concerning the eternal Son-ship of Christ. He thought Christ was the Son of God only in respect of his *human* nature. And therefore, (he said) when he taught his children their catechism, he taught them only to say, that Christ is the Son of God, but not that He is the *eternal* Son of God, (as others were wont to instruct their children) for he supposed that He was not God's Son before His incarnation. I did from the Scriptures reason with him, and endeavored to convince him how great an error he was in. He seemed to receive some satisfaction, and did with many tears declare unto me that he had for some time been afraid lest his error in judgment should be fundamental and so his soul perish. I shall conceal the person's name; he was not only a church-member, and an aged professor, but of special note and improvement in the town where he lived. He is since dead, (and I hope at rest) for he was not obstinate in his error but willing to receive light.

---

[10] John Owen, *Works of John Owen, The Glory of Christ* (Edinburgh: Banner of Truth, 1965), 1:287.

Now if such a man were in the dark concerning so great an article of faith, I doubt not that there are many among us who need information and confirmation in the doctrine of Christ.

The way to be preserved from apostasy in hours of temptation is to be well settled in principles. Nor is anything of greater concernment to the souls of men. Hence Pareus[11] did exceedingly rejoice when he had completed his explication of Ursin's catechism, saying: "Now Lord, let your servant depart in peace since I have lived to finish what I so much desired." And he professed that he looked upon all his other books as unprofitable compared with that. A great divine said of Luther's Catechism, "that one little book is a gem to be valued above six thousand worlds." But especially to have the loins of the mind girt[12] about with those principles of truth which concern the person and office of Christ, has a tendency to confirm believers in faith and holiness, which is the thing that I have been willing to aim at.

As for the manner of handling what is here delivered, it would have been easy to have discoursed on such mysterious subjects, after such a metaphysical strain as none but scholars should have understood anything, but in so doing I should neither have pleased God nor edified the souls of many among you.

The most learned and pious Dr. Usher did, even in Oxford itself, deny such Corinthian vanity. And in a sermon preached to a great and princely auditory, he has this notable passage:

---

[11] David Pareus (1548–1622) was a German reformed teacher and Biblical commentator. He taught at the University of Heidelburg in the 17th century and was well known for his explication of the Heidelburg Catechism.

[12] Securely fastened.

"Great scholars (said he) may think it stands not with their credit to stoop so low, but let the most learned of us all try whenever we please, we shall find, that to lay this ground work right, that is, to apply ourselves to the capacity of the common auditory, and to make an ignorant man understand these mysteries in some good measure, will put us to the trial of our skill, and trouble us a great deal more, than if we were to discuss a controversy or handle a subtle point of learning in the schools."[13]

I have in these, as well as in other sermons, endeavored to make the truth plain and easy to be understood, hoping that both the learned and unlearned among you may reap some benefit thereby. I have been with you now for the space of more than 25 years, during all which time, the Lord Jesus knows what my difficulties have been. But the mercy I have enjoyed in the advantage for service which God has graciously favored me with, has more than compensated for all my outward afflictions and pressing oppressing temptations; especially considering that I have had an opportunity of speaking to the world not only in the pulpit, but by the press, and by means thereof, to leave something behind me, (a thing which I have a 1,000 times prayed for) which (I trust in Christ) will be of use to some of God's elect, when I shall be seen no more. And in which thing I hope I may use the apostle's expression, and say, I have not sought my own profit, but the profit of many that they

---

[13] James Usher, *A Brief Declaration of the Universality of the Church of Christ, and the Unity of the Catholic Faith Professed Therein Delivered in a Sermon Before His Majesty King James I* on the 20th *of June, 1624* (London: University of Michigan Ann Arbor online library, 1624), 34–35.

might be saved. But in a more peculiar manner I have designed your edification.

And I will confess to you that no subjects ever insisted on by me have had so much of my heart as these which I now present unto you; the most of which were, as you may remember, preached some years ago; only the last discourse was more lately delivered. That concerning the Deity of Christ was preached when I handled the body of theology. That concerning his Son-ship fell in my course as I went over the second chapter of the Revelation. All the other were sacramental meditations on Christ. There are sundry[14] among you who have been blessed with not only a religious, but a learned education, being by your relations designed for the special service of God in the gospel of His Son. I can give you no better advice than this, above all things, study Jesus Christ. You may know much in the tongues and arts (as the devils do) yes, and have a doctrinal historical knowledge of Christ too, and yet not savingly know the truth as it is in Jesus. But then you will be very unfit to teach others. I commend unto you the serious perusal of the books written by those honorable men of God, Dr. Thomas Goodwin,[15] and Dr. John Owen,[16] in whose writings there is more of the spirit of the gospel and of the mystery of Christ than in the books of any authors in the world that I know of. They are voluminous, and in many places very profound, and in those respects not so proper for the ordinary sort of readers

---

[14] Several.

[15] Thomas Goodwin, *The Heart of Christ in Heaven Towards Sinners on Earth* (Edinburgh: Banner of Truth, 2015); *Christ Set Forth* (Edinburgh: Banner of Truth, 2015).

[16] John Owen, *The Glory of Christ* (Edinburgh: Banner of Truth, 2012); *The Death of Death in the Death of Christ* (Edinburgh: Banner of Truth, 1999).

to converse with. But such of you as are scholars may be greatly edified by them.

And unto you all, I cannot give a better exhortation than that where-with the apostle concludes his last epistle: "Grow in grace and in the knowledge of our Lord and Savior Jesus Christ. To him be glory both now and forever Amen!" (1 Pet. 3:18).

So prays your ever-loving (though unworthy) teacher,

Increase Mather
October 25, 1686

# 1
# There Is a Covenant of Redemption

---

"When you shall make His soul an offering for sin,
He shall see His seed."
Isaiah 53:10

It has been observed by some that, of all the prophets, Isaiah is the most evangelical. Nor is there any part of his prophecy that has more of the gospel in it than this fifty-third chapter; wherein he speaks as if he wrote rather a history than a prophecy. He speaks as if he had lived in the days of the gospel and been an eye-witness to the sufferings of Christ and to the glory which followed. In this verse the death of Christ is set forth from the grounds, and also from the effects of it.

    1. From the grounds from whence it came to pass. Firstly, from the *pleasure* of the Almighty, "It pleased the Lord to bruise Him, He hath put Him to grief." Secondly, another ground of the sufferings of Christ is the *covenant of redemption*, which was between God and Christ concerning the salvation of the elect: "When you shall make His soul an offering for sin"; according to the Hebrew, the words run thus: "If He shall put His soul an offering for sin" [*IM-TASIM*]. Which words evidently imply a compact or glorious agreement between God the Father and the Son, about this matter. The prophet in the ninth verse had declared the innocency of Christ, "He had done no

violence, neither was any deceit found in His mouth." But then it may be said, why was the Lord pleased to bruise Him? How could that stand with justice? Answer: Because there had been a voluntary agreement between God and Christ concerning this matter; Christ undertaking to do the work of a redeemer, and to satisfy the demands of justice, and so it might please the Lord to bruise Him, and no injury done neither. But then there must be another cause assigned as procuring the sufferings of Christ. Therefore, thirdly, the sins of the elect were the procuring cause thereof. "He made his soul an offering for sin." Not any sin of His own, which He was absolutely free from, but the sins of His people.

2. The death of Christ is here described from the glorious *fruits* and *effects* of it: namely, the meriting of conversion and salvation on the behalf of His elect, which is intimated in that expression of "seeing His seed."

There are three doctrines which we may take notice of from the words:

Doctrine 1. That *there is a covenant of redemption.*
Doctrine 2. That *the sins of the elect were the procuring cause of all those sufferings, which Jesus Christ was exposed unto.*
Doctrine 3. That *Jesus Christ by His death has merited the conversion and salvation of his elect.*

### There is a covenant of redemption[17]

We have formerly spoken of the covenant of grace made with believers. There is some difference between that and this of redemption, which is the subject of our present discourse; in that

---

[17] John Flavel, *The Works of John Flavel, Vol. 1: The Fountain of Life* (London: Printed for W. Baynes and Son, 1820), 52-62; Samuel

the federates[18] are God and the believer, in this the federates are God and Christ. In that, the condition was free and absolute; in this, the condition is subjection to the law, yes, to the penalty of the law. In that, the promise was life and glory. In this the promise is a name above every name. So then there is some difference between the covenant which God made with men concerning Christ, and which He has made with Christ concerning men.

This is a glorious mystery, and the knowledge of it is purely scriptural and evangelical. We shall endeavor by the help of Christ to set before you what the scripture speaks concerning this mystery, in sundry propositions which may serve to explicate and demonstrate the truth before us.

**Transactions between the Father & Son**
There have been eternal federal transactions between God the Father and the Son concerning the redemption of the elect. This proposition is expressive of the nature of the covenant of redemption, showing what it is. And there are three things contained therein.

---

Rutherford, *The Covenant of Life Opened, or, A Treatise of the Covenant of Grace* (Edinburgh: Printed by Andro Anderson for Robert Brown, 1655), 290–302; Samuel Willard, *The Doctrine of the Covenant of Redemption* (Boston: Printed by Benjamin Harris, 1693); Jonathan Edwards, *Observations Concerning the Scripture Economy of the Trinity* (New York: Charles Scribner's Sons, 1880); Herman Bavinck, *Reformed Dogmatics, Vol. 3: Sin and Salvation in Christ* (Grand Rapids: Baker Academic), 212–216.

[18] Two parties who are joined together in union with one another.

*1. There has been a transaction between the Father and the Son concerning the redemption of the elect*
It is true, that there were transactions and consultations concerning mankind, before man was made. "God said, let us make man in our image after our likeness" (Gen. 1:26). Who are the persons here spoken of, as creating man? Even the Father, Son, and Spirit. For none but the Lord alone did or could create man. So then, the sacred Trinity did as it were sit in council concerning the creation of man, but besides that, there have been glorious transactions between the Father and the Son concerning the work of redemption. Thus, some interpret that Scripture in Zechariah 6:13, "The counsel of peace shall be between them both" as being between the Lord Jehovah and Him that is called the Branch. God and Christ did (as it were) consult together how peace and reconciliation might be obtained for sinners, so as might consist with the honor of justice. Hence Christ is called God's companion: "Awake O sword against the man that is My Fellow" (Zech. 13:7). Now companions are wont to consult together.

*2. This transaction was from eternity*
For God from eternity knew that man would fall, and though it be true that neither the divine prescience nor anything else is or can be a cause of God's will (which is Himself) either electing or reprobating, nevertheless, we may from that consideration argue and conclude that He did from eternity contrive a way for man's recovery. It is true that the revelation of this contrivance was not before time. It was first discovered presently after the fall (Gen. 3:15) and it was not put in execution until the "fullness of time came" (Gal. 4:4) that is to say, when the Son of God became incarnate. Nevertheless, the thing was

## Covenant of Redemption

agreed upon, by the Father and the Son before the world began, we may see by those Scriptures, namely, 2 Timothy 1:9 and Titus 1:2.

### 3. *This transaction was federal*

It was managed and concluded in a covenant way; there was a glorious compact or agreement between the Father and the Son about this matter. For whatever is required to a complete formal covenant, we may see here. For example, where there is a covenant there are two distinct persons, as it is said, "A mediator is not of one" (Gal. 3:20). There must be more persons than one, where there is a mediator; so such a covenant as we are speaking of is not of one person. Thus, the Father and the Son are two distinct persons, although essentially one, yet personally two. Again, covenants are *voluntary* transactions; so it is here, God the Father was voluntary therein, for He might have chosen whether He would have accepted of satisfaction for sin from any but the sinner himself. It was not any necessity of nature, but an act of His holy will and pleasure, to propound terms of reconciliation. The Son was likewise voluntary in this matter; for He might have refused to have accepted the terms of this covenant, but it pleased Him to accept thereof. Moreover, where there are terms and articles of agreement accepted of, on both parts, there is a proper covenant. So it is here (as afterwards will appear) God says unto His Son, "if you will become a redeemer of my elect, you must go into the world, and take on yourself the nature of man, and in that nature do and suffer all that is needful to be done in order to salvation." "*I will do it all*," says Christ. Here now is a glorious covenant.

## God has made glorious promises to Jesus Christ

God has made glorious promises to Jesus Christ, on condition of His undertaking the work of a redeemer. For example, God has promised that He should be every way fitted and qualified for that undertaking, and therefore that a human nature should be created for Him, so that He might be in a capacity for the management of that undertaking: "A body hast thou prepared me, O God" (Heb. 10:4). And that gifts and graces of the Holy Spirit should be poured upon Him, according to that great and unparalleled undertaking: "He was anointed with the oil of the Spirit above his fellows" (Ps. 45:7). Yes, "He received the Spirit not by measure" (John 3:34) (i.e. above measure); there are no known limits set to that portion of the Spirit which Christ as man received. It is a higher expression than can be used concerning any man or angel, or creature, but only is it spoken concerning Christ who is more than a man or creature.

Also, God promised to assist Him in His work, "Behold my servant whom I uphold" (Is. 42:1), and verse 4: "He shall not be discouraged, till He has set judgment in the earth." This is that which encouraged Christ in His work notwithstanding the difficulties and sufferings, which he was on the account thereof exposed unto (Is. 50:7, 9). And God promised Him blessed success in His undertaking, even, "that the pleasure of the Lord should prosper in His hands," as the context expresses. Yes, success in respect of those He undertook for, that His elect should be converted, and therefore "He shall see His seed." Yes, not only the elect among the Jews, but the Gentiles also.

Therefore, look into the 49th chapter of Isaiah, where this covenant of redemption which we are now discoursing of is likewise intimated. In the two first verses Christ speaks of His

## COVENANT OF REDEMPTION

call to the work of a redeemer; in the third verse there is a promise that the elect *Jews* should be converted to Christ. Nay but says Christ (v. 4) I must have more than that, my blood is of greater value than to be given for them *only*. Those that make bargains, begin low at first, so God bids Christ low comparatively at first, (you must always remember that these things are spoken after the manner of men, so that we might be able to conceive and understand something of these mysteries). Well, says the Lord, if that be not enough, you shall have more, if the conversion of the Jews be not enough, elect Gentiles shall be converted also. "And now says the Lord that formed me from the womb to be his servant, to bring Jacob again unto him—Is it a light thing that you should be my servant to raise up the tribes of Jacob, and to restore the preserved of Israel? I will also give you for a light to the Gentiles" (Is. 49:5-6). Again, the justification of believers is promised to Christ. In this context, it is promised that "He should justify many," and their *sanctification*: "by the which will we are sanctified through the offering of the body of Jesus once for all" (Heb. 10:10). What will is that? That will has respect to the covenant of redemption, even the will of God concerning Christ's coming into the world to do the work of a redeemer. The sanctification of believers does originally flow from thence. And their eternal salvation was promised to Jesus Christ. God promised that incase Christ would become subject unto death, all believers on Him shall receive an everlasting inheritance (Heb. 9:15).

There are also promises made to Christ of victory over all His enemies (Is. 50:9, Ps. 100). Yes, over death itself (Ps. 16:9). God promised that if Christ would become subject to death, in order to the salvation of his elect, He should not continue long in that state of death, but should have a glorious resurrection to life and immortality. Therefore, well might the apostle say, "it was impossible for Him to be held under the pains of death" (Acts 2:24). And God promised that a glorious reward should be given to Him, as we see in the last verse of this chapter. And accordingly, God has exalted Jesus Christ to sit at His own right hand, and has made not only men but angels and authorities and powers subject to Him, because He has been obedient unto death, even the death of the cross. Therefore, God has exalted Him, and given Him a name above every name, that at the name of JESUS every knee shall bow in heaven, and in the earth, and under the earth (Phil. 2:9-11).

## Jesus has accepted His undertaking

Jesus Christ the Son of God has accepted of this undertaking according to the terms propounded by the Father. Hence it is that God is styled the God of Jesus Christ; and the Lord of Christ, (Ps. 16:2, 45:7; Mic. 5:4; John 20:17; Eph. 1:17; Rev. 3:12) namely in respect of the covenant. As the Lord is said to be the God of believers in respect of the covenant of grace; so He is said to be the God of Christ in respect of the covenant of redemption. On this same account also, God is said to be greater than Christ, (John 10:28, 14:28). In that by voluntary dispensation, Christ has taken upon Him the work and office of a redeemer, and is become subject to the Father therein; and thence also is said to be His *servant* (Is. 52:13). Yes, His *willing* and *obedient* servant: "The Lord God has opened mine ear and I was not rebellious, neither turned away my back" (Is. 50:5). And if we call to mind the terms of the covenant of redemption but now hinted at, we shall see the truth of this. One article of it was that the Son of God should become incarnate; hence Christ in respect of His incarnation is said to be "sent of God"

(Rom. 8:3). Now this the Son of God did readily comply with, "Sacrifice and offering you have not desired, but a body have you prepared me; then said I, Lo, I come, (in the volume of your book is it written of me) to do your will, Oh God" (Heb. 10:5, 7). The Son of God there speaks, "Father, (he says) is it your will that I should go into the world, that I should assume the human nature, and in that nature do the work of a redeemer? If that be your will, Lo, I come to do your will, O God."

Again, according to the articles of agreement in this covenant, the Son of God was to become subject to the law, and this article he has complied with, "God sent His son, made of a woman made under the law" (Gal. 4:4). So that the eternal Son of God has condescended not only to become incarnate, to be made of a woman, (although that condescension was infinite) but also to be made under the law, and this not only the *general* (or *moral*) law, which all mankind, yes, all rational creatures are subject unto, and Christ has exactly observed (Matt. 5:17), but also that *special law* of the Church wherein He was born. Hence He was circumcised, baptized, and kept the Passover, and subjected to other rites of the Jewish Church, which were then of divine institution (Matt. 3:15), and also the *singular law* of a redeemer which is expressed in the text. Namely, that "He shall make His soul an offering for sin." If Christ would become a redeemer, He must subject Himself to the penalty of the law, He must yield *passive* as well as *active* obedience. This is there called the commandment of the Father, John 14 ult. "and the Father gave me commandment." And this has Christ complied with and submitted to, "Christ has redeemed us from the curse of the law, being made a curse for us" (Gal. 3:13). Yes, and He was willing and hearty in this compliance, His heart was in it (John 10:18).

### God and Christ observe the terms of the covenant

Yes (to speak after the manner of men, and with humility and reverence) they hold each other to the agreement which has been between them. The Father holds Christ to the terms of the covenant, He has bated[19] Him nothing of what He engaged to perform, "God spared not his own Son" (Rom. 8:32). Nor did Christ ever desire to have any abatement thereof, which would be derogatory from the glory of God (John 12:27). Christ does also hold the Father to what He has promised, and therefore, we do find Him professing to the Father that He does expect that He should be as good as His word, "Father, I have glorified you on the earth, I have finished the work which you gave me to do, and now, Oh Father, glorify me with your own self, with the glory which I had with you before the world was" (John 17:4-5). It is as if Christ should say, "I have done the work of a redeemer, and now I expect the wages of a redeemer, according to the covenant which has from eternity been between us." Yes, Christ holds the Father unto what He had promised not only concerning Himself, but also with respect unto all that shall believe on Him, as in verse 24 of that chapter: "Father, I will that they also whom you have given me, be with me where I am, that they may behold my glory." The Father has promised that it should be so, and now Christ does will and demand it should be made good.

---

[19] Restrained.

## COVENANT OF REDEMPTION

**God and Christ confide in one another**
They do as it were take one another's word. The Father trusts Christ. Hence the patriarchs and saints which lived before the coming of Christ were saved, "They without us were not made perfect (Heb. 11:40). They were not brought to heaven in one way and we in another, but were saved by the merit of Christ as well as we. But how could that be, since Christ had not died before their souls were saved? Well, but God took Christ's word for it, that He would in the fullness of time go into the world and die for them. Hence the death of Christ was effectual before it was actual. He is said to be "the Lamb slain from the foundation of the world" (Rev. 13:8). How was Christ slain from the foundation of the world? Not only in respect of the decree of God, but in respect of the efficacy of Christ's death. For the death of Christ was efficacious ever since the first believer that ever lived in the world, and this was because the Father took the word of the Son concerning His coming into the world to do the work of a redeemer. Also, Christ has taken God's word. Hence He came and died before such a time as half of the elect were saved, or had any actual being in the world. In the Old Testament, the Father did trust the Son, in the New Testament the Son does trust the Father.

**Glorious ends in the covenant**
God and Christ had glorious ends, in making this covenant of redemption. The great and ultimate end was His own glory. Not that there could be any real access[20] or addition of glory beyond what He always had; but only a discovery of that glory. Hereby the glory of the divine attributes is manifested (e.g. The

---

[20] Archaic way of saying increase by addition.

sovereignty of God). That God should elect some and reprobate others, and find out a way for the salvation of fallen men but not of fallen angels, is a glorious manifestation of the absolute sovereignty of Him who is God most high. And the glory of His justice is also here to be seen. The apostle insists upon that: "To declare His righteousness" (Rom. 3:25-26). Indeed if God had pardoned sin without satisfaction, mercy had been seen, but then God would not have had the glory of His justice. Likewise, divine grace is hereby glorified, "according to His grace which was given us in Christ Jesus before the world began" (2 Tim. 1:9). Herein God commends His grace, in that he should be contriving a way, and such a way, to bring us to salvation before the world began. And the grace of the Lord Jesus was exceeding abundant, in that when man had dashed himself to ruin, and the everlasting Father was coming out against him with arrows dipped in blood, that now the Son of God should step in and undertake to satisfy justice. And the wisdom of God is also hereby discovered to saints and angels, "the mystery which from the beginning of the world hath been hid with God, to the intent that now to the principalities and powers in heavenly places might be made known to the Church the manifold wisdom of God" (Eph. 3:9-10). And the truth is that nothing but infinite wisdom could have contrived such a way as this for accomplishing of salvation, where justice and mercy so meet together, and "righteousness and peace do kiss each other."

**Word of consolation to those in the covenant**
First, it is a comfortable consideration to think on the ancient love of God. If you are concerned in this covenant, God loved you before ever you loved Him; yes, before ever you had any

## Covenant of Redemption

being; your name was written in the Lamb's Book of Life before the foundation of the world, even from all eternity. Therefore, David says, "Remember, O Lord, your tender mercies and your loving kindnesses, for they have been from of old" (Ps. 25:6). God has had designs of grace towards you, from everlasting.

Second, if you are concerned in this covenant GOD who has an absolute dominion over his creatures, has given you to Jesus Christ, "Yours they are and you gave them me, and all mine are yours, and yours are mine" (John 17:6, 10). God has given you to Christ to redeem and save you. There is such a poor creature I give him to you, take him, save him, bless him forever, says the Lord.

Third, hence your salvation is certain. As sure as the covenant of redemption, as sure as that Christ has made His soul an offering for sin. This is a suitable meditation to be in the heart at the time of receiving, when we are at the Lord's Table. Is there bread and wine here? As sure as this is bread and wine so sure is it that Christ has died, and so sure it is that you shall be saved, and behold the glory of Christ in Heaven, if you are one concerned in this covenant of redemption. You will say, this is comfortable if I did but know that this belongs to me; How shall I know that?

**Answer 1.** *Do you believe on Jesus Christ?* No man can know his interest in this covenant before he does believe. Have you a heart purifying, a heart sanctifying faith? Have you accepted of Jesus Christ upon His own terms? Has God given you to see the glorious loveliness and excellency of the Son of God, so that there is none in heaven, nor any on the earth whom you desire in comparison of Him? Have you received Christ as Prophet, Priest, and King? Then this belongs to you.

**Answer 2.** *Are you the seed of Christ?* Have you become His child in respect of spiritual regeneration? "If any man be in Christ, he is a new creature (2 Cor. 5:17). Have you a new heart, a new head, a new tongue, a new life and all? Are you become the workmanship of God created in Christ Jesus to good works? If so then this belongs to you.

**Answer 3.** *Have you felt the blessed power and efficacy of the death of Christ in your own soul?* Is sin mortified in your soul through the blood of Christ? And is your soul mortified to the world thereby? Then this belongs to you. Can you say after the blessed apostle, "By the cross (i.e. the death) of the Lord Jesus Christ I am crucified unto the world, and the world unto me" (Gal. 6:14)? If sin be indeed mortified in your soul, then Christ has made His soul an offering for your sins.

# 2
# Jesus Christ Is the Son of God

"The Son of God."
Revelation 11:18

In the second and third chapters of the Revelation, we have those seven epistles which the Lord Jesus Christ sent from heaven to the churches in Asia. These words are part of that which is in order the fourth of these epistles, the preface whereof is contained in this verse, which does signify:

1. The *person* to whom this epistle was written, namely, the *angel* or principal officer in the Church of Thyatira.

2. The *author* or *sender* of it, namely, Jesus Christ, who is here described,

   i. From His *relation* unto God the Father, whose Son he is.
   ii. From His *omniscience*, He has eyes like a flame of fire.
   iii. From His *omnipotence*, His feet are like fine brass.

At present we shall only speak to the first of these, namely, that relation which Christ does sustain towards God, and the doctrine to be insisted on, is: *That Jesus Christ is the Son of God.*

Now in the doctrinal handling of this great foundational truth we shall, first, lay down some propositions for explication. And, second, mention some arguments for demonstration.

## A personal respect

Christ is said to be the Son of God in a personal respect. Not His *essence* but His *person* is begotten of the Father. Christ is said not to be the Son of God in respect of His *human* nature. It is a sure principle of truth, *filiation* is of the *person*, not of the *nature*. Christ in respect of His human nature is styled "the Son of Man" (Matt. 16:13), but not the Son of God; for He was the Son of God before the assumption of His human nature. "God sent His Son into the world" (John 3:17). Therefore, He was the Son of God before His coming into the world. "The Son of God was manifested" (1 John 3:8). Now *manifestation* is of that which was extant before. So that the *person* of Christ did exist before He was manifested in the flesh. Agur lived many ages before the human nature of Christ did actually exist, yet he acknowledges that God had a Son (Prov. 30:4). Yes, and so did Nebuchadnezzar (Dan. 3:25). Christ is said to be "the Son of the Father" (3 John 3), when the human nature was from the Holy Ghost (Matt. 1:18). If Christ were the Son of God in respect of His *incarnation*, He should be the Son of the Holy Ghost rather than the Son of the Father, when the Scripture speaks otherwise, calling Him only the Son of the Father: "He is the only begotten of the Father" (John 1:14); not begotten of the Holy Ghost. To *beget* is the relative property of the Father, to *be begotten* is the relative property of the Son. Christ's being the Son of God is a proof of His being equal with God (John 5:18). When if He were the Son of God in respect of His human nature, or considered as mediator, that would be no proof of His equality with God, for on these accounts He is inferior to and not equal with the Father (John 10:28). Nor is Christ said to be the Son, or to be *begotten* in respect of His Godhead absolutely considered, for then every person in the Godhead should be so. Christ is not said to be the Son of the *Godhead*, but the Son of *God*, where God is taken personally for God the Father. The divine nature absolutely considered is from *itself*, (i.e. from *none other*),[21] but the Son of God is from *another* (i.e. from the *Father*). He is *God of Himself*, but not a *Son of Himself*. He receives not His *being* from the Father, but only His *personality*. The Son of God is a divine person begotten of the Father.

### By divine ineffable generation

Christ is the Son of God by divine ineffable[22] generation. That divine generation which the Sonship of Christ does intimate is *ineffable*. As it is said in another respect, "who can declare his generation?" (Is. 53:8). So as to this generation, who can declare it? Yet must we know and believe that the Son is begotten of the Father. The Scripture (which is the ground of faith in all divine mysteries) is clear for this (John 3:17). If Christ be the Son of God after a higher manner than the angels, He is so in respect of *divine generation*. But He is the Son of God after a higher manner than the angels, "unto which of the angels said He at any time, 'You are my son?'" (Heb. 1:5). Christ is so the Son of God as no one else is, and therefore, is said not only to be *begotten*, but the *only* begotten Son of God: "We beheld His

---

[21] This is, in short, the doctrine of divine aseity. The word aseity comes from the Latin a—"from" and se—"self." For further reading on this doctrine see: James Dolezal, *All That is in God* (Grand Rapids: Reformation Heritage Books, 2017), 11-17; Stephen Charnock, *Discourses on the Existence and Attributes of God* (Edinburgh: Works of Stephen Charnock, Vol 1, 1864), 374-419; Herman Bavinck, *Reformed Dogmatics, Vol. 2* (Grand Rapids: Baker Academic, 2004), 148-159.

[22] Too great to express or describe with words.

glory, as the glory of the only begotten of the Father" (John 1:14).

There are sons of God in respect of creation: so Adam was the Son of God (Luke 3 ult.). There are sons of God in respect of adoption; so all believers are the sons of God. (John 1:12; Gal. 4:5). There are sons of God in respect of imitation and similitude; so the holy angels are styled sons of Elohim (Ps. 89:6; Job 38:7). And Godly men are styled His sons, because they bear His image, and are in some measure like Him, as children are like their Father (Matt. 5:45; Luke 6:35; Eph. 5:1). Wicked men are called the Devil's children on the same account of likeness and imitation (1 John 3:10). And there are sons by nature, so Christ alone is the Son of God. See what is written in Exodus 23:20-21, "I send an angel before you, to keep you in your way, and to bring to the place which I have prepared: obey His voice, and provoke him not—for my name is in Him." That angel of the Lord is indeed the Lord of angels; Jesus Christ the increated[23] angel of the everlasting covenant. God's name is in Him, because He is God's Son. As a Son has the name and nature of his Father belonging to him; so has Christ the name and nature of God in Him. Hence, He is said to be God's own Son (Rom. 8:3). God "sent His own Son" [*ton heautou Huion*] the Son of Himself and in the 32$^{nd}$ verse of that, chapter it is said, "God spared not His own Son" [*ho idios Huios*], meaning His Son in a proper or a natural sense. And God is said to be Christ's *own* Father (John 5:18). And therefore, is He (as but now was intimated) said to be equal with God, "He thought it not robbery to be equal with God" (Phil. 2:6). If Christ had not been God's own Son, for Him to have given out that He was *equal with God*

---

[23] Not created; uncreated.

would have been the greatest robbery and sacrilege that ever was. If He were only the adopted son of God, that would not prove His equality with the Father. But an own son (though he may be inferior, or it may be superior to his father in respect of office, or on other accounts) in respect of nature he is equal with his father. A son is not of an inferior nature to his father. Christ (then) is God's Son as to nature, therefore, His Son in respect of generation.

**The generation of the Son of God is eternal**
The generation of the Son of God is eternal. They err fundamentally who imagine that the Son of God had no existence before His incarnation. The world was created about four thousand years before the Son of God came into it, nevertheless He made the world (John 1:3, 10). Therefore, He did exist before He became a man. God had many adopted sons in the days of the Old Testament, therefore, He had an own Son for whose sake they were adopted. The Jews do sometimes call the *Messiah* by that name of [*Jinnon*][24] which signifies a Son, and is the word used Psalm 72:17 which place may be thus read, "before the sun, Jinnon is His Name," intimating that the generation of the Son of God was from eternity, even before there was any sun in the firmament or any creature that had a being, yet then the second person in the Trinity is the Son of God. All other generations have a beginning and ending, but this has neither, "You are my son this day have I begotten you" (Ps. 2:7). That day as it has respect to Christ's being manifested in the sight of Heaven and Earth to be the Son of God, is to be applied to the

---

[24] This word occurs only once in the Bible in Psalm 72:17. The Jews traditionally understood this word as a proper name for the Messiah.

time of His resurrection; but as it respects Christ's generation, it is to be understood concerning the day of eternity. God's day is eternity. There is no yesterday nor tomorrow with Him, but an infinite now, which never goes away.

The Scripture does expressly declare that the generation of the Son of God is an eternal generation. Wherefore wisdom (that is Christ the eternal essential wisdom of the Father) has said, "The Lord possessed me in the beginning of His way, before His works of old, I was set up from everlasting, from the beginning, or ever the earth was. When there was no depths I was brought forth, when there were no fountains abounding with water; before the mountains were settled, before the hills was I brought forth. While as yet He had not made the earth, nor the fields, nor the highest part of the dust of the world... Then was I by Him, and I was daily His delight, rejoicing always before Him" (Prov. 8:22-26, 30). What can be more plain to prove that the generation of the Son of God is eternal? See also what is spoken by the prophet Micah, "You Bethlehem Ephrata—out of you shall He come forth, that is to be ruler of Israel, whose goings forth have been from of old, from eternity" (Mic. 5:2). So that there are two goings-forth of Christ there spoken of, one out of Bethlehem in respect of His birth, the other from the days of eternity in respect of that generation we are discoursing of. Hence also it is said, "In the beginning was the Word" (John 1:1). Those words do allude to the first words in the Bible, and they show that Christ was when the world first began. It is not said that Christ was made then (as it is said in Gen. 1:1 that "In the beginning the heavens and the earth were made") but that He was then. The Son of God had real existence when the world began to be created. Now, there was nothing but eternity before the world began.

Once more, the Son of God is styled, "the brightness of His Father's glory" (Heb. 1:3). The sun and that brightness, that refulgency,[25] or beaming forth of light which proceeds therefrom, are coetaneous.[26] So God the Father and the Son are *co-eternal*. The Son is only in order of nature and not in time before the beams issuing therefrom; so is God the Father only in order of nature and not in time before God the Son. Had it been possible for the sun in the firmament to be eternal, the beams and brightness thereof would have been eternal too. Thus, inasmuch as God the Father is eternal, the Son of God, who is the brightness of His glory, is eternal also.

**A spiritual & intellectual generation**
The generation of the Son of God is a spiritual and an intellectual generation. God is a Spirit, and therefore, all carnal imaginations about this generation are to be abhorred. This divine generation concerning which we speak, is by the infinite understanding of God reflecting upon his own beauty, and conceiving an image of Himself. Hence Christ is called the "image of God" (Col. 1:15). Not an *accidental*[27] but *essential* image; as the son does bear the image and nature of his father. Divines are wont thus to express it, "God may be considered as understanding and knowing Himself, that is God the Father, and as understood and known by Himself, that is God the Son." And the Scripture does set forth the generation of the Son of God by such expressions as show that it is spiritual and intellectual

---

[25] Brightness, brilliance, splendor, etc.
[26] From the Latin word "coeval." Having the same age or date of origin.
[27] The term "accident" refers to an attribute that may or may not belong to a subject without affecting its essence.

(e.g. He is called the "wisdom of God" (1 Cor. 1:24). Now wisdom is of the understanding.

Again, Christ is called the "Word of God" (Rev. 19:13; 1 John 5:7). Now there is not only a sensible word which is pronounced, but intelligible word which is brought forth in the understanding. Words are the birth of the understanding. So the Son of God is begotten by the infinite understanding of the Father.

**Distinct but one**
Though God the Father and the Son are personally distinct, they are essentially one. Therefore, the Son is called "the express image of His person" (Heb. 1:3). If a man see an angel, he may behold the image of God, His wisdom, goodness, and power but not the express image of His person. But he that sees the Son of God, sees the person of the Father in His Son; yes, the character (as the Greek has it) of his person. A son is sometimes very like his father, the picture of his father, and so the image of his person; but never any son so like the father, as the Son of God is like His Father. There is an essential likeness of God in Christ "who being in the Form of God" (Phil. 2:6). The Father and the Son are personally two. "I (says Christ) am not alone, but I and the Father that sent me," and in verse 18, "I am one that bears witness of myself, and the Father that sent me bears witness of me" (John 8:16, 18). Where there is one sending, and another sent, there are two distinct persons. And two witnesses are two persons; so are God and Christ; yet are they essentially one: "The Father and I are one" (John 10:30). If they were not essentially one, there would be more Gods than one, which is heresy and blasphemy to imagine.

## A Wonderful & incomprehensible mystery

The generation of the Son of God is a wonderful and incomprehensible mystery. That particular insisted on in the former proposition, manifests the truth of this. That two persons should be essentially one! That more persons than one should be in the same individual nature! Among created beings it is not so, nor can it be. They that differ personally have not the same individual being, but God the Father and the Son have the same indivisible essence. A father and a son have the same generical essence, but not the same numerical essence, but God the Father and the Son have so. And how wonderful is it to consider, that there should be a father no older than his own son, and an own son no younger than his own father! And how wonderful is it, that the same person should be both God and man! So is Christ. In that vision to which my text has reference, He is called "the Son of man" (Rev. 1:13-14), and here "the Son of God," because He is both God and man in one person. That there should be more natures than one in the same individual person, is *wonderful*.

These are glorious mysteries that we should with humble adoration think of. With these propositions explaining the truth before us, we proceed in the second place, to mention some arguments demonstrating, that Jesus Christ is the Son of God. Briefly;

### *Argument 1: Testimony given to the sonship of Christ*

We may argue from that testimony which has been given to the Sonship of Christ. Even Christ's greatest enemies have been forced to confess this. The Devil once cried out, "What have I to do with you, Jesus you Son of God most High!" (Luke 8:28). And we have upon record in the Word of God, the testimonies which those that knew Christ have given to this great truth. John Baptist says, "I saw and bear record, that this is the Son of God" (John 1:34). Nathaniel also said to Him, "Rabbi, you are the Son of God" (John 1:49). Peter in the name of all the disciples, professed, "We believe, and are sure that you are Christ the son of the living God" (John 6:69). And an archangel from heaven said to the virgin Mary, "that holy thing which shall be born of you, shall be called the Son of God" (Luke 1:35). Christ Himself bore witness to this truth, concerning his own Sonship, "do you say of Him whom the Father sanctified and sent into the world, 'You are blaspheming,' because I said 'I am the Son of God?'" (John 10:36). And God from heaven has preached this truth; "At the time when Christ was baptized, lo, a voice from heaven saying, 'this is my beloved Son, hear you Him'" (Matt. 3:17). Also at His transfiguration, unto which the Apostle Peter has respect when he says, "We were eyewitnesses of His majesty, for He received from God the Father honor and glory, when there came from the excellent glory (i.e. from God, whom the Hebrews are wont to call by the name of glory) 'this is my beloved Son in whom I am well pleased:' and this voice which came from heaven we heard when we were with him in the holy mount" (2 Pet. 1:16–18).

*Argument 2: the miracles at Christ's passion*
From the miracles which happened at the time of Christ's passion. I do not mention the sufferings of Christ to prove His relation to God. His state of humiliation was the great objection which the Jews had against His being the Son of the Blessed. Hence Christ became a rock of offence to them that would not believe that he was the Son of God except, "He came down from the cross" (Matt. 27:42–43). So the heathen world;

What! He be a God that was crucified! They thought that incredible. But there were such miracles attending the sufferings of Christ, as did plainly manifest that He was none other but the Son of God. From the sixth to the ninth hour of the day, there was darkness all the land over. This was no ordinary eclipse of the sun, for it was at the full of the moon, being at the Passover, which ordinary solar eclipses, we know, are at the new moon. Moreover, the veil of the temple was torn in two, from the top to the bottom; and the earth did quake, and the rocks rent, and the graves were opened, and bodies of saints which slept arose. These solemn providences were so convictive as that the captain who commanded the soldiers the day that Christ was crucified, cried out, "Truly, this was the Son of God. Oh the Jews have killed the Son of God" (Matt. 27:45, 51-52, 54).

*Argument 3: the resurrection & exaltation*
From the resurrection and exaltation of Jesus Christ. He was declared to be the Son of God, by the resurrection from the dead (Rom. 1:4). Christ said that He was the Son of God before He suffered on the Cross; now if He had not been so indeed, we may be sure that God would never have raised Him out of His grave. Also, Christ raised Himself: "Therefore, did He say to the Jews, 'destroy this Temple, (meaning the Temple of his Body) and in three days I will raise it up'" (John 2:19).

Nor would God have exalted Him so as He has done, even to sit at His own right hand, had He not been His own Son: "For unto which of the Angels said He at any time, sit—at my right hand?" (Heb. 1:5). God has exalted Him very highly "giving Him a name above every name" (Phil. 2:9). And we may therefore conclude, that Jesus Christ is the Son of God.

*Argument 4: the voice of Christ.*
From the powerful quickening voice of Christ. "The words (says Christ) that I speak, they are spirit and life" (John 6:63), and verses 68-69, "You have the words of eternal life." Peter might well therefore add, "we are sure you are the Son of God" (Matt. 16:16). God is known by His voice, "Have you an arm like God? can you thunder with a voice like Him?" (Job 40:9). "The voice of the Lord is powerful, the voice of the Lord is full of Majesty; the voice of the Lord breaks the cedars, the voice of the Lord divides the flames of fire" (Ps. 29:4-5, 7). So is the Son of God known by His voice: "The hour is coming, and now is, when the dead shall hear the voice of the Son of God, and they that hear shall live" (John 5:25). Certainly, He that can by His voice make the dead to live is more than a mere son of man, *He is the Son of God.*

Let me conclude this doctrine with a word of *exhortation*, and there is a three-fold exhortation before us:

## 1. Endeavor after knowledge & good understanding in this glorious mystery

*Consideration 1. That there are but few that have this knowledge.*
At least not in that degree and measure which ought to be; yes and which might be, considering the means which are plentifully afforded. As the apostle speaks to the Hebrews, "When for the time you ought to be teachers, you have need that one teach you again which be the first principles of the oracles of God" (Heb. 5:12). It is marvelous to consider what ignorance is in many that call themselves Christians. As a holy man once complained, (not without too much cause) that Christ is but

little known amongst Christians. Yes, some that are very knowing in other matters of religion, yet if they be examined about Christ, they are found exceeding ignorant.

*Consideration 2. The surpassing excellency of this knowledge.*
Hence the apostle says, "Yes doubtless I count all things but loss, for the excellency of the knowledge of Christ Jesus my Lord" (Phil. 3:8). Knowledge is an excellent and desirable thing. Knowledge of the creature is so, which caused Solomon to say that "wisdom excels folly, as far as light excels darkness" (Ecc. 2:13). Much more is the knowledge of Christ excellent and desirable, whereby all other knowledge is sanctified, and without which all other knowledge will never save a man's soul. Hence the holy prophets of old were very diligent in endeavoring after this knowledge; as we see: "of which salvation the prophets have enquired, and searched diligently, searching what, or what manner of time the spirit of Christ which was in them did signify, when it testified beforehand the sufferings of Christ, and the glory that should be revealed" (1 Pet. 1:10-11). Nay the blessed angels admire and seek after this knowledge. The things of Christ are things which the angels desire to look into. And if prophets, if angels have desired to search into the mystery of the incarnation of the Son of God, much more into that of His eternal generation. The truth is, that this knowledge is not had but by divine revelation. Christ is not known by the light of nature, but by the special revelation of the Holy Ghost, held forth in the gospel. Wherefore the apostle says, "It pleased God to reveal his son in me" (Gal. 1:15). And when Peter made that glorious confession, "You are Christ, the Son of the living GOD," it was said unto him, "Flesh and blood has not revealed it unto you but my Father which is in heaven"

(Matt. 16:16-17). Hence the whole doctrine concerning Christ is called a mystery: "you may understand my knowledge in the mystery of Christ" (Eph. 3:4). A mystery is a divine secret which is not known but by revelation; so is the truth concerning Christ. And as all truths which reveal Christ are excellent; so there is a special excellency in those which concern the person of Christ.

*Consideration 3. That though this knowledge be excellent and rare, yet it is attainable.*
That is to say such a measure thereof as is necessary in order to salvation. Indeed, a comprehensive knowledge of this mystery concerning the Sonship of Christ is not to be attained by any man or creature. There are many external works of God which we are not able to comprehend. If we look into the works of creation we soon see more than we can comprehend. "Do you know about the layers of the thick clouds, the wondrous works of Him that is perfect in knowledge?" (Job 37:16). So concerning the works of providence, "Oh the depth of the riches both of the wisdom and knowledge of God! How unsearchable are his judgments and his ways past finding out!" (Rom. 11:33). Much less can we comprehend the immanent and eternal works of God such as election and reprobation, and such as that which is implied in the text respecting the eternal generation of the Son of God. The most knowing in the world must needs confess his own ignorance when such mysteries are spoken of. As Zophar said to Job, "Oh that God would show you the secrets of wisdom, they are double to that which is! Can you by searching find out God? Can you find out the Almighty unto perfection? What can you know?" (Job 11:6-8). And David confesses with respect unto a knowledge far less

mysterious than what we are speaking of, "Such knowledge is too wonderful for me, it is high I cannot attain unto it" (Ps. 139:6). Yet such a knowledge of Christ as is necessary unto salvation may be had, especially in these gospel times, when that promise is eminently fulfilled— "they shall all know me, from the least of them to the greatest of them" (Jer. 31:34). Such a knowledge of Christ as is essential to salvation, every true believer has. The gospel does reveal Christ much more clearly than ever the law did. Hence it is said, that "he that is least in the kingdom of heaven (i.e. the least minister of the gospel) is greater than John Baptist" (Luke 7:28), not in respect of degrees of grace, but as to a more clear and abundant discovery of Christ. There is no minister of the Gospel, but knows more of Christ than John Baptist did, that is to say, he knows more concerning His passion, resurrection, ascension, sitting at the right hand of God, coming to judge the world, than John was acquainted with (Matt. 11:11).

*Consideration 4. That ignorance about Christ in these days of gospel light, is exceeding dangerous.*
A man had better be ignorant of everything than of Christ. It is said, "My people are destroyed for lack of knowledge" (Hos. 4:6). If any ignorance be destructive, ignorance of Christ is so. Men may know much in divine things and yet perish, because they do not know Christ. So the Pharisees, they had great knowledge in the letter of the Scripture, and yet because they knew not Christ they perished to eternity. "This is life eternal, to know you the only true God, and Him whom you have sent, Jesus Christ" (John 17:3). Then they that remain ignorant of Christ, must needs be in danger of death, yes of eternal Death.

By way of *direction* here observe these rules:

Rule 1. If we would have a right understanding in those truths which concern the person of Christ the Son of God, *we must attend the means which the Lord has appointed in order to the attaining that knowledge.* For example, searching the blessed Scriptures: Therefore, Christ said, "search the Scriptures for they testify of me" (John 5:39). And Solomon shows, that the way to know wisdom is to seek and search after it (Prov. 2:4). We must dig and dive into the rich mines of Scripture. In things of this nature, we must take heed of our own conceits, but be sure to keep close to the Scriptures. And attendance to the word preached is also the way to gain and grow in the knowledge of Christ. For it is the great work of the ministry to preach Christ, to open the mysteries of Christ. We read in Genesis 29:3, how "the shepherds rolled the stone from the well's mouth, and watered the sheep;" so ministers are to open the mysteries of Christ and salvation by Him. The Lord does bestow gifts of knowledge upon some above others for this end in special, so that they might be fitted for the work of the ministry and might bring to the knowledge of the Son of God, (Eph. 4:13). Prayer also is a means to attain this knowledge: "If you cry after knowledge and lift up your voice for understanding, then you shall find the knowledge of God" (Prov. 2:3, 5). We should pray for the illumination of the Spirit, and the rather because the Lord Jesus has promised to send His Spirit to guide us into all truth (John 16:13). Let us be earnest in prayer that we may receive that unction from the Holy One that shall make us know all things that are necessary to be known in order to our salvation and consolation.

Rule 2. *Beware of presumption and curiosity*. We must not be wise above what is written. It is good to enquire into these divine and holy mysteries, so far as God has revealed, but no further. If we do, not knowledge but blindness will be the effect of those enquiries. A vehement object we say destroys the sense. If men come too near the sun, their eyes are dazzled that they cannot see. A moth by approaching too near the light destroys itself; so many a proud presumer by too boldly prying into these glorious mysteries has destroyed his own soul.

## 2. Believe that Jesus Christ is the Son of God

It is not so easy a matter to believe this as many think for reason cannot comprehend this mystery, and thence it is not easy after a right manner, with the heart to believe it. Yet it is necessary to be believed, as being a fundamental principle in religion. Therefore, when Peter in the name of the disciples professed that "Christ is the Son of God, " the Lord replied, "upon this rock I will build my church" (Matt. 16:18). So then they that do not believe this, do not belong to Christ, nor to the Church of Christ. All religion, yes *whole Christianity* would fall to the ground if this principle should be plucked up. The sum of the gospel is contained in this great truth. Hence Paul's preaching is summarily expressed by saying, "He preached Christ that He is the Son of God" (Acts 9:20). There are many truths of lesser concern, which through ignorance may be disbelieved or denied, and yet a man's salvation not hazarded thereby. But it is not so as to this truth respecting the Sonship of Jesus Christ; whosoever disowns it, will miss of eternal Salvation. "Whosoever denies the Son, the same has not the Father" (1 John 2:23). Hence Satan has made it his great design to oppose this Truth. The Devil said to Christ, "IF you be the son of God"

(Matt. 4:3). The wicked Devil would feign have that questioned. Wherefore in the days of the apostles, he stirred up Ebion[28] and Cerinthus,[29] and other heretics who denied the deity, and so the eternal Sonship of Christ, which is thought to be the occasion of John's writing his Gospel wherein he does most plainly and abundantly assert the Godhead of Christ. Afterwards, Satan stirred up Arius,[30] who maintained that Christ

---

[28] Ebion was a heretical teacher and founder of the group known as the *Ebionites*. Tertullian is the first early father to write against Ebion and he did so on the basis that Ebion taught that Jesus was merely a man and not divine. Tertullian placed Ebion in the 2nd century while early Church father Jerome believed Ebion to be a 1st century contemporary of John the Apostle. More can be read on Ebion's errors in Tertullian's works *Against Heresies* and *De Carne Christi* found in: A. Cleveland Coxe, *Ante-Nicene Fathers. Vol. 3: Latin Christianity: It's Founder, Tertullian, I. Apologetic; II. Anti-Marcion, III. Ethical*, ed. Alexander Roberts and James Donaldson (New York: Christian Literature Publishing Company, 1885), 536–537, 542, 651. Irenaeus also briefly mentions Ebion in his work *Against Heresies* found in: A. Cleveland Coxe, *Ante-Nicene Fathers. Vol. 1: The Apostolic Fathers, with Justin Martyr, Irenaeus* ed. Alexander Roberts and James Donaldson (New York: Christian Literature Company, 1885), 361–362.

[29] Cerinthus was a first-century heretical teacher who believed and taught Gnosticism. Similar to the Ebionites, he taught that Jesus was merely a man and not divine. Irenaeus stated that Cerinthus believed Christ was not born of the Virgin Mary but was the natural son of Joseph and Mary and that Christ descended upon Jesus at his baptism but left him at the crucifixion. See: Irenaeus, *Against Heresies* found in: A. Cleveland Coxe, *Ante-Nicene Fathers. Vol. 1: The Apostolic Fathers, with Justin Martyr, Irenaeus* ed. Alexander Roberts and James Donaldson (New York: Christian Literature Company, 1885), 361–362.

[30] For more information on the errors of Arius, see Philip Schaff, *Nicene and Post-Nicene Fathers: Series II, Volume 4: Athana-*

was only a creature and not the eternally begotten Son of the Father; and the Church was in danger of being 'carried away with that flood' of Arian heresy which overwhelmed the world (Rev. 12:15). "The whole Christian world" (as one of the ancients speaks) "sighed and wondered to see itself become an Arian."[31] Thus we see Satan lays battery against this truth, because he knows the souls and salvation of men are concerned in the belief of it. Therefore, let us firmly believe it.

By way of Direction, here remember these two Rules:

Rule 1. We must set this down for a principle, *that we are to believe beyond reason*. Albeit the great truths of the Christian religion are not contrary unto, yet they are above reason. Therefore, we must believe what we are not able to comprehend. Pagans of old, were wont scoffingly to call the Christians *Credentes*, that is *believing persons*, because they were such as would believe beyond the comprehension of reason. And one reason why Socinians[32] in these late days have had such gross

---

*sius: Select Works and Letters* (Grand Rapids: Christian Classics Ethereal Library, 1891), 16-72, 334-335, 385-531, 731-1168. Justo Gonzalez also has two helpful chapters titled "The Arian Controversy and the Council of Nicea," and "The Arian Controversy After Nicea" in the first volume of his work titled *A History of Christian Thought* (Nashville: Abingdon Press, 1987), 261-290.

[31] This quote is attributed to Jerome— "The world groaned to find itself Arian" Philip Schaff, *Nicene and Post-Nicene Fathers: Series II, Volume 6: Jerome: Letters and Select Works* (Grand Rapids: Christian Classics Ethereal Library, 1894), 738.

[32] Socinians deny the doctrines of the Trinity, propitiatory atonement, the eternal generation of the Son of God, and original sin; though they are most well known for their ardent denial of the Trinity. For a helpful treatment of this heresy, see John Owen, *The Works of John Owen, Vol. 12: The Gospel Defended* (Edinburgh: Banner of Truth, 1966).

and damnable mistakes about the person of Christ, has been because they would not believe beyond reason; which the great and glorious mysteries respecting the Sonship and the eternal generation of Christ's person are beyond what any man's reason can fathom. Therefore, we must set faith on work, and though we cannot conceive how this or that should be, yet we are to take divine testimony for it. Take the Word of God for it that it is so, and there rest satisfied.

Rule 2. *Let us not content ourselves with a mere notional belief about this matter; but see that our faith be sincere and cordial.* Let us see that this truth be not only in our heads but in our hearts also. If men have only a notional belief concerning this, that is no more than what the devils have. "You believe that there is one God, you do well, the devils also believe and tremble" (Jas. 2:19). So do the devils believe, that Jesus is the Son of God, and tremble at the apprehension of His infinite majesty. A whole legion of devils fell a roaring at the presence of the Lord Jesus, crying, "Jesus, you Son of God, are you come to torment us before the time?" (Matt. 8:29). But hearty belief of, and closure with this truth is another thing. Philip said, "If you believe with all your heart, unto him that professed, I believe that Jesus Christ is the Son of God" (Acts 8:37). That is necessary in order to salvation: "With the heart man believes unto righteousness, and with the mouth confession is made unto SALVATION" (Rom. 10:10). When a man does so believe this truth, as that he could gladly lay down his life for confessing and bearing witness to it, that is hearty believing. As in the primitive times it was as much as a man's life was worth to confess this truth. The infidel Jews and heathen of those days would be ready to kill anyone that should profess such a belief.

In which respect the apostle might well say "Whosoever confesses that Jesus Christ is the Son of God, God is in him, and he in God" (1 John 4:15). This is to be understood, not of a mere notional but of a cordial, yes and a practical believing. We proceed therefore, to:

### 3. Practice according to this truth

Let everyone look to it, that they carry towards Christ as becomes towards the Son of God.

Question: *How is that?*

Answer 1. *Attend to whatever He shall say.* That may be the special reason why Christ in the preface of his epistle to the church in Thyatira, mentions His being the Son of God, namely, so that He might stir up attention. And if Christ has anything to say to us, we may be sure that it is well worth the hearkening to, because He is the Son of God. "Hear, for I will speak of excellent things, and the opening of my mouth shall be right things, for my mouth shall speak the Truth" (Prov. 8:6-7). Oh then hearken to the Son of God! The Father of Glory has said from heaven, "This is my Son, hear Him" (Matt. 3:17). It is as much as a soul is worth not to regard what Christ the Son of God shall say. "It shall come to pass, that every soul that will not hear Him shall be destroyed from among the people" (Acts 3:23).

Answer 2. *Love the Lord Jesus Christ.* Certainly, we do not carry towards Christ as becomes towards the Son of God, if we do not love Him. For He is the loveliest person, that we can set our hearts upon. "He is altogether lovely" (Song 5:16). Nor can we love God except we love Jesus Christ. Everyone that *begat*, loves him that is *begotten* also. He that loves the father will love the son that is like the father. Oh how vile are they that do not love Christ! What a dreadful Scripture is that, "If any man love not the Lord Jesus Christ, let him be ANATHEMA.[33] MARANATHA"[34] (1 Cor. 16:22). If any man live and die without love in his heart towards the Lord Christ, he will be *cursed*, yes and the curse will remain upon him until the Lord Jesus shall come to judgment.

Answer 3. *Honor Jesus Christ the Son of GOD*. When God sent His Son into the world, He said, "They will reverence my Son" (Matt. 21:37). Sure it is, that upon that account reverence and honor is due unto Him. Christ considered as the Son of God, does partake in the same nature with the Father, and so is equal with God, and thence is to have equal honor with Him. "The Father has committed all judgment to the Son, that all men should honor the Son, as they honor the Father" (John 5:22-23). It is storied concerning the Emperor Theodosius,[35] that at a time when he was too favorable to the Arians, he made a decree that as much respect should be put upon his son as upon himself; and a godly minister whose soul hated the Arian heresy coming into the emperor's presence, did him great obedience, but took no notice of his son, at which the emperor was highly displeased. "Oh, (says the minister) cannot you bear it, that less honor and respect should be given to your son than is manifested towards yourself, and do you think the God of

---

[33] Accursed.

[34] Come, Oh Lord!.

[35] Emperor Theodosius I lived from 347-395 AD. He ruled as emperor of the Roman Empire from 379-395 AD. In 380 AD he issued an edict that made the Nicene creed the universal creed for establishing orthodoxy in the Christian Church. In 381 AD, he called the Council of Constantinople in an effort to suppress Arianism.

heaven will bear it at your hands, that you should give less honor to His Son Jesus Christ than you do unto God Himself?" At the hearing of which words, the emperor was stricken with conviction, and after that was no more so favorable to the Arians. God requires men and angels to worship His Son Jesus Christ, which is the greatest honor that can be put upon any object: "When he brings the first begotten into the world, he says, let all the Angels of God worship Him" (Heb. 1:6). And this is certain, that they, that will not honor the Son of God now, shall be fain to honor Him one day, when they shall see Him come down from heaven in all His glory. Then shall every knee in heaven, and on earth, and under the earth "bow at the name of JESUS" (Phil. 2:10), and every tongue shall confess that Jesus Christ is Lord, to the Glory of God the Father.

Answer 4. *Believe on the Lord Jesus Christ.* Since He is the Son of GOD, He is the object of faith. You believe in God, (says Christ to His disciples) believe also in me. And it was said unto the man that was born blind, *Do you believe on the Son of God?* We may safely venture our souls upon HIM. Indeed, if He were only the Son of *Man*, it would be dangerous and destructive to put the trust and confidence of our souls in Him, but since He is the Son of *God*, we may and must do so.

The Lord has therefore, revealed the truth, so that we may be encouraged in believing. "These things are written that you might believe that Jesus is the Christ the Son of God and that believing you might have life through His name" (John 20:31).

Know it, (yes, you that live under the gospel cannot but know it) that there is no SALVATION but by CHRIST, and there is no salvation by Christ but in a way of believing on Him. "He that believes on the SON has everlasting life, and he that believes not the Son, shall not see life, but the wrath of God abides on him" (John 3:36). And having faith, let us live the life of faith, so that we may be able to say after the blessed apostle, "I live, yet not I but Christ lives in me, and the life which I now live in the flesh, I live by faith on the Son of God" (Gal. 2:20).

# 3
# JESUS CHRIST IS OVER ALL, GOD BLESSED FOREVER

"Who is over all, God blessed forever."
Romans 9:4

The apostle having in the preceding chapters of this epistle, handled the doctrine of justification, he proceeds in this (with several other chapters following) to discourse concerning the mystery of predestination. He had before asserted, that the elect of God could not perish; against which assertion it might have been objected, that the Jews who were an elect nation perish in their infidelity. To this he answers, that not elect but reprobate (whether amongst Jews or Gentiles) are the persons that shall fall short of salvation.

In the beginning of this chapter, Paul expresses his exceeding great sorrow, for the unbelief of the Jews, and for their being thereupon rejected of God. And he mentions several things which were the springs and aggravations of his sorrow. One thing that made him grieve the more, was that the Jews were his *brethren* and *kinsmen*, and therefore, their misery could not but go more near to his heart. Another thing which aggravated his grief, was the consideration of those peculiar privileges and glories which are to be affirmed of the Jewish nation. Two of which are mentioned in this verse:

1. *Theirs are the Fathers.* They were descended from those blessed patriarchs, Abraham, Isaac, and Jacob. Now it is a very sad thing to consider, that the children and posterity of those blessed ancestors, should become the subjects of so great misery and ruin as is now come upon the Jews.

2. *Of them, as concerning the flesh, Christ came.* Christ was as to His human nature an Israelite, which is the greatest glory the Jewish nation can speak of; and therefore, that is mentioned in the last place. Christ came of them only in respect of His flesh, in other words, His body or human nature. He has another nature which did not come of them but is eternal.

Words cannot be expressed which do more clearly and fully declare the Godhead of Christ than these do. And therefore, let the doctrine from them be in the words of the apostle.

Doctrine: *That Jesus Christ is over all, God*

It will be good for us to be established in this great truth, the firm belief whereof is necessary in order to salvation. The argument which the Scripture affords for the confirmation of this fundamental principle in the doctrine of Christ, may be reduced to four heads.

## 1. The names and titles which are peculiar to God, are in the Scripture given to Jesus Christ

For example, He is expressly and frequently called God, and that not only in the New Testament but in the Old. It is said that "the angel spoke unto Jacob, saying, I am the God of Bethel" (Gen. 31:11, 13). Now, God the Father is nowhere styled an angel, but that angel who is the God of Bethel was none else but Christ the uncreated angel of the everlasting covenant. Again, when Jacob blessed Joseph's children, he thus expressed himself, "God before whom my fathers Abraham and Isaac did walk, the God which led me all my life long unto this day, the Angel which redeemed me from all evil, bless the lads" (Gen. 48:15-16). This Angel is called *God*, and the *redeemer*, which is God's title (Is. 47:4). The words cannot be applied unto any created angel, for Jacob prayed for a blessing from Him, as the author of redemption from all evil. This then clearly proves that Christ *is God*, and that Jacob did so believe.

And Job was of the same faith, "In my flesh shall I see God, whom I shall see for myself, and mine eyes shall behold" (Job 19:26-27). God the Father cannot be seen with *bodily* eyes; He is the *invisible God*. The divine nature cannot be seen, but Christ by reason of his being flesh, may be seen; and at the latter day every eye shall behold Him. Then shall Job (and everyone else) in his flesh see God. Now Christ is not said to be God in respect of similitude, as angels are; or in respect of office, as magistrates are; but in respect of nature. Christ Himself argued against the Jews, that it was necessary that the Messiah should be God in another and a higher sense than the kings of Judah (who were but types of Him) are styled Gods; and therefore, God by nature (John 10:35). Hence, He is said to be the *true God*: "We are in him that is true, even in his son Jesus Christ. This is the true God, and eternal life" (1 John 5:20).

We may not affirm concerning any other man, but only the man Christ Jesus, that He is the true God. He is also styled the *Mighty God* (Is. 9:6), and the *great God* (Titus 2:13), which titles cannot without blasphemy be given to any mere man or creature (Deut. 10:17). Again, that glorious and fearful name Jehovah is peculiar unto him who is the only true and living God, "that men might know that you whose name alone is Jehovah, are the most high over all the earth" (Ps. 83:18). Yet that very name is frequently in Scripture given to Jesus Christ the Son of God. Jehovah says, "They shall look upon me whom they have pierced." He that pours a spirit of grace upon the house of David (which none but God can do) says, "they have pierced me" (Zech. 12:10). See also (Gen. 16:10, 13; 18:16-17; 22:11-16) in all which Scriptures Christ the Son of God has the name of Jehovah given to Him. And in the New Testament Christ is described by a name which answers the name *Jehovah*, for He is there said to be, "He which is, and which was, and which is to come" (Rev. 1:8), which words are an interpretation of the name Jehovah.

Again, that name *Ehjeh*, or as it is in English *I AM*, is proper to God, "you shall say to the Children of Israel, I AM has sent me unto you" (Ex. 3:14). But this name belongs to Jesus Christ the Son of God; who therefore said, "before Abraham was I AM" (John 8:58). Whence the blinded Jews thought that Christ had blasphemed, because He being a man attributed to Himself the proper title of the eternal God. And that title of the *Lord of Glory* is peculiar to God. "Who is the King of Glory? The Lord of Hosts is the King of Glory" (Ps. 24:10). But Jesus Christ is so. "The princes of this world crucified the Lord of Glory" (1 Cor. 2:8). He then is the Lord of Hosts. And that title of the *Most High*, may not be given to any besides God. "None but He is the Most High over all the earth" (Ps. 83:18). But Christ is the *Most High*; therefore, He is in the text said to be God over all, that is to say, God Most High; a style fit for none but the true God only. And Scripture says of Him that "He is above all" (John 3:31). He is above the patriarchs, above the prophets, above Moses, yes above all creatures. He is *Lord of all*, and therefore God.

## 2. The essential incommunicable attributes of God belong to Christ[36]

There are some attributes whereby the nature of God is in part discovered, which creatures do partake of, such as mercy, goodness, wisdom, holiness, righteousness, etc. Albeit these excellencies are not in the creature in such an eminent manner and infinite degree as they are in the creator. But there are other divine attributes which are incommunicable to any creature, being the absolute properties of the divine nature. Now these are affirmed concerning Christ the Son of God. For example, eternity is an essential incommunicable attribute of God. He is the eternal God. Yes, eternity itself (Is. 57:15). But Christ is in respect of His divine nature eternal. Hence John Baptist said that Christ was *before* him, as well as *after* him. Before him in respect of His divine nature, though after him in respect of His human nature (John 1:15). "He was before Abraham" (John 8:58). "He was with God before he became flesh," (John 6:62) yes, "before the world began" (John 17:5). "Even from everlasting" (Prov. 8:23; Mic. 5:2). "He is before all things" (Col. 1:17). To signify His eternity, He appeared unto John with, "His head and His hairs white like wool, and as white as snow" (Rev. 1:14). Eternity is that which has neither beginning nor end of days which is true concerning the Son of God (Heb. 7:3). "He is Alpha and Omega, the Beginning and the End, the First and the Last" (Rev. 22:13).

Again, *omnipresence* is an incommunicable attribute or property of the divine nature. None but God is or can be in *all* places at same time. But this is true of Christ. And therefore, at the same time when He conversed with men in this world, it

---

[36] See: Herman Bavinck, *Reformed Dogmatics, Vol. 3: Sin and Salvation in Christ* (Grand Rapids, Baker Academic, 2006) 308-316.

was said of Him, "He is in heaven" (John 3:13). And "He is present in all places where His servants are gathered in His name" (Matt. 18:20). And "He walks amongst his Churches everywhere" (Rev. 2:1).

And *omniscience* is peculiar unto God; He is *perfect in knowledge*. But so is Christ. "Therefore, Peter said to him, 'Lord, you know all things'" (John 21:17). It is God's prerogative to search and know the hearts of the children of men. Solomon in his prayer at the dedication of the temple said unto God, "you only know the hearts of the children of men" (1 Kings 8:39). Yet this is most truly affirmed of Christ: "He needed not that any should testify of man, for He knew what was in man" (John 2:25). The Scripture says that "the Son of God has eyes like a flame of fire" (Rev. 19:12), (i.e. like lightning), to note that His eyes see what is in the hearts of men; for these flames of fire reach unto the bowels and pierce the inside. And He says, "all the Churches shall know that I am He which searches the minds and hearts" (Rev. 2:18, 23). By this argument was Nathaniel convinced of the deity of Christ. When he perceived that the Lord Jesus looked upon him while he was alone and no mortal eye beheld him, he concluded that this Jesus must needs be the *Son of God, the King of Israel*. But thus for the second argument.

## 3. Divine worship belongs to Christ

God alone is the object of religious worship: "You shall worship the Lord your God and Him only shalt you serve" (Matt. 4:10). But such worship is due to Christ. Therefore, Joshua fell on his face and did worship when Christ appeared unto him as the captain of the host of the Lord (Josh. 5:14). And the wise men of the east "fell down and worshiped Him" (Matt. 2:11).

## Over All

And the disciples when they saw that he was more than a mere man, "they came and worshiped Him saying, 'of a truth you are the Son of God'" (Matt. 14:33). Therefore, we read of the *servants* (i.e. *worshipers* of Christ) (James 1:1; Rev. 1:1; 22:3). And men are commanded to "kiss the Son of God" (Ps. 2:12), which *kissing* implies *adoration*. Hence idolaters were wont to kiss their idols which were worshiped by them (1 Kings 19:18; Job 31:27).

A little further to enlarge here, *baptism* is a religious ordinance; and Christ is the object of it (Acts 2:38). Christ is indeed the institutor of all religious ordinances, and therefore, the object of religious worship. Baptism, the Lord's Supper, the Christian Sabbath, He is the Lord of those holy institutions, and thence is religiously acknowledged in them all. Again, an oath is a religious thing; so that it is unlawful to swear by any creature. But when a man is called to take an oath, he may solemnly invocate the name of Christ. For so did Abraham (Gen. 22:15-16), and so did Paul in the beginning of this chapter, "I say the truth in CHRIST I lie not." Prayer is a part of religious worship. But Christ is an object of prayer. "Jacob wept and made supplication unto Him" (Hosea 12:4). Stephen, when dying prayed unto Christ to receive his soul (Acts 7:59). All the disciples in Jerusalem called upon the name of Christ (Acts 9:21). Yes, all true believers are described to be such as "call upon the name of Jesus Christ our Lord" (1 Cor. 1:2). Once more, believing is an act of internal worship. No creature may be believed on. Cursed is he that puts his trust in man. But Christ is the object of faith (John 14:1). The apostle says, "I trust in the Lord Jesus Christ, In Him shall the Gentiles trust" (Rom. 15:12). Often in the Scripture we are commanded not only to believe Christ, but to believe in Him, and to believe on

Him; which if He were not God we might not do. Yes, Christ is the blessed object of the eternal praises of saints and angels. Therefore, He is here said to be "God blessed forever," which is also a description of the true God (Rom. 1:25) unto whom everlasting praises are due. The host of heaven worship Him saying, "blessing be to the Lamb for ever and ever" (Rev. 5:13).

### 4. The proper works of God belong to Christ

There are *immanent* acts of God. Election is so and that is ascribed to Christ (Matt. 24:31). None but God can say of all that do or ever shall believe, that they are His elect. And there are external works of God which cannot be affirmed of any other. For example:

(1) The work of *creation* is peculiar to God, "I am the Lord that makes all things, that stretches forth the heavens alone, that spreads abroad the earth by myself" (Is. 44:24). No finite or second being ever was or can be the author of a work of creation. But Christ is so. "All things were made by Him, and without Him was not anything made, that was made" (John 1:3). Words cannot be more express and full than those are; declaring Christ the Son of God to be the creator of the world. Hence He is said to be "the beginning of the creation of God" (Rev. 3:14), not that He was the first creature, as Arius did most corruptly interpret, but because the creation of God did receive its beginning from Him.

(2) To *preserve* and *govern* the whole creation is the proper work of God (Neh. 9:6). None but one of infinite power and wisdom is able to govern the world. One of the ancients speaks truly in saying that, "If God should give unto any one of His creatures all the wisdom that is in all the angels in heaven, and then commit the government of the world to him, but for one

hour, he would bring all to confusion and ruin in an hour's time." But Christ upholds and governs the world. "By Him all things consist, and are upheld by the word of his power" (Col. 1:17; Heb. 1:3). And therefore it is said, "He works hitherto" (John 5:17), namely as to that work of preserving and governing all things which He has made.

(3) To *forgive sin* is the proper work of God. The Pharisees, held a true principle (though by them misapplied) when they maintained, that none can forgive sin but God only (Mark 2:7; Mic. 7:18). But it belongs to Christ to do this (Ex. 23:21; Matt. 9:6).

(4.) The *sending of the Holy Ghost*, is a work peculiar unto God. It is high blasphemy to say that any mere man or creature has power to send the Holy Ghost. But this is most true of Christ. He says, "I will send the Comforter, He shall glorify me, He shall receive of mine and shall show it to you" (John 16:7, 14). Hence the apostle speaks of "the supply of the Spirit of Jesus Christ" (Phil. 1:19). None but God can bestow the gifts and graces of the Holy Spirit, yet these does Christ confer upon whom He will, and in what degree and measure he will. "He baptizes with the Holy Ghost and with fire" (Matt. 3:11). Therefore, He is God.

(5) *Miraculous works* are proper unto the great God to effect. "Blessed be the Lord God who only does wondrous things" (Ps. 72:18). Nothing less than the arm of omnipotency can produce a miracle. But Christ was the author of many miracles, the like whereunto were never wrought in the world (Matt. 9:33). As for the holy prophets and apostles, they were not the authors of those miracles which were wrought by their hands. But Christ was Himself the true author of the miracles wrought by Him. Hence when the apostles wrought miracles,

they did it in the name of Christ; as in Acts 3:12, 16 and 9:34, which, if Christ had not been God, they could not have done. But He did miracles in His own name and by His own power: "I will, be you clean" (Matt. 8:3).

(6.) To *raise the dead* is the work of God. Which may be one reason why He is styled *the living God.* It is God and none else that raises the dead. But Christ is the author of the resurrection. "As the Father raises up the dead, even so the Son quickens whom he will" (John 5:21). "He raises up believers on Him, at the last day" (John 6:40). Therefore He said, "I am the resurrection and the life" (John 11:25). No mere man or creature can say so. It is then necessary that we should know and believe that *Jesus Christ is over all, God blessed forever.*

The great objection which the Jews make against this glorious truth is, that *Christ is a man, and therefore cannot be God.* But we must believe that Christ is God and man too, both God and man in one person. The Jews themselves dare not say that God is not able to take a human nature into personal union with Himself. And if God in His word has declared that He has done this wonderful thing, woe be to that man's soul that will not believe Him. The Scriptures of the Old Testament which the Jews own to be the word of God, expressly testify that a man should be in the world who is God's equal, and therefore, God and man in one person: "Awake, Oh sword against My Shepherd, against the man that is My Fellow, says the Lord of hosts" *(*Zech. 13:7). The Jews crucified Christ because He being a man said he was the Son of God, and so equal with God. Yet their own prophets had spoken of such a man as should be fellow to the Lord of hosts.

The chief objection which Socinians make against this article of faith is, that the Father is said to be greater than Christ (John 14:28). If Christ be inferior to God, how then is He in respect of nature God?

Answer: One may be inferior to another in respect of office and yet equal to him in respect of nature. A son in respect of office may be inferior (or superior) to his father; so Christ as mediator is inferior to the Father, and yet in respect of nature is equal to Him, and one with Him.

## If Christ be God, then He is a fit person to be a savior and mediator for sinners

The salvation of the elect proceeds from the mediatorial office of Christ, in respect whereof, He is a prophet, priest, and king. Our redemption does not depend merely upon this, that there is one given to be a prophet, priest, and king of His Church, but that such a one as is God, is the person vested with those offices. For if any other person in the world (if any mere man or creature) had been constituted a mediator for sinners, none would have been saved by him. The power and efficacy of Christ's office, whence it does become effectual to salvation, arises from His being God blessed forever. He has undertaken and discharged His office not merely as man, but as God over all.

Christ could not have been such a prophet as He is had He not been God. For He was to be a prophet to the whole Church in all ages and in all places of the world. Christ as man while He was on earth did personally declare the mind of God to Jews, being made a minister to that Church (Rom. 15:8), but His prophetical office was not confined to them. The Church never was without a prophet since the world began, nor ever shall be, and this prophet is Christ. And therefore, Christ was said to be sent of God, (as prophets are) before His incarnation. The LORD of hosts, that by the shaking of his hand can destroy the nations, was sent of God, (Zech. 2:8). It was necessary that Christ as prophet should have a full comprehension of the mind and will of God which no mere creature was capable of. "No man has seen God at any time, the only begotten Son who is in the bosom of the Father He has declared Him" (John 1:18). No man, no not Moses himself, the greatest prophet, has seen God or lain in his bosom so as to know all that is in his heart. This is peculiar unto CHRIST who is God blessed forever. The prophets and preachers in the days of old were inspired by the Spirit of Christ. Noah was so (1 Pet. 3:19), and all the holy penmen of the Bible were so (1 Pet. 1:21). It was necessary in order to Christ's being the great prophet of the Church, that He should have power to send the Holy Spirit to illuminate the minds of His elect (John 16:13-14; 1 Cor. 2:10, 16). Christ as man has not this power; but being God over all, He was a fit person to undertake this glorious office.

And Christ being such a person as is God, is the reason why His priestly office was effectual unto salvation. He is such a priest as did by one offering perfect forever them that are sanctified, which if he had not been more than a man could never have been. "The blood of Christ who through the eternal Spirit offered Himself shall purge the conscience" (Heb. 9:14). If that offering had not been sanctified through the eternal Spirit, it could not have purged the conscience. All the sufferings of the human nature of Christ would not have expiated the guilt of sin, if Christ had not an eternal Spirit (i.e. a divine nature), which caused the sufferings of His other nature to be infinitely meritorious. The blood of Christ is the blood of God, and therefore, it has an infinity of value and worth in it; so as to be able to purchase redemption and eternal salvation for all that shall obey him.

And the reason why Christ is a fit person to be the Church's, head and king is because He is God over all. His government is not only eternal, but internal in the hearts and consciences of men. If Christ would undertake to be the king of the Church, it was necessary that He should influence the hearts of believers, and that He should subdue their corruptions, and that He should vanquish death, which things a mere man could never do. So Christ's fitness for the work of a mediator, does depend upon his being over all God blessed forever.

## Let every one of us give to Jesus Christ that which is due to God

As it is said in Psalm 29:1-2, "Give unto the Lord, Oh you mighty, give unto the Lord glory and strength, give unto the Lord the glory due unto His name; Worship the Lord in the beauty of holiness." So let us do to Christ. We are to honor Jesus Christ, as much as we honor God Himself; for He is God. The Father will not be offended but well pleased with us if we do so. He would have "all men to honor the Son even as they honor the Father" (John 5:23). Your heart is God's due. He says give me your heart. Let Christ have your heart, give your whole heart to Him, that He may rule as God there. Give your soul to Jesus Christ. None of us may bequeath our souls to any but unto God; yet unto Jesus Christ we may bequeath them, as dying Stephen did, who said, "Lord JESUS receive my spirit" (Acts 7:59). Let us love Jesus Christ with such a love as is due to none but God. Love Him with all your heart, with all your soul, and with all your mind and with all your strength. And

Grace be with all them that love our Lord Jesus Christ in sincerity. Amen. To HIM be glory both now and forever,
AMEN.

# 4
# JESUS CHRIST THE SON OF GOD, IS MAN AS WELL AS GOD

"The Word was made flesh."
John 1:14

John wrote his gospel after the rest of the evangelists. When the apostles were most of them dead, there arose certain heretics who denied the Godhead of Christ. This is thought to be the occasion of John's writing his gospel; so that he might bear witness against that which was the grand error of the time wherein he lived. He does most plainly assert and prove the deity of Christ; for which cause he has been commonly styled John the Divine. And that is in a special manner the scope of this chapter, which does contain a description of the person of Jesus Christ, in respect of both his natures *divine* and *human*. The divinity of Christ is asserted and proved from verses 1 to 14. His human nature is declared in this verse and in these words; wherein we have:

1. The person assuming, called "the Word" (i.e. the Son of God or second person in the Trinity, who is called "the Word"). In the Old Testament Christ is called the Word when David said before God, "For your Word's sake you have done all these great things" (2 Sam. 7:21). His meaning may be that all was done for the sake of Christ. And the Jews of old were

wont to term the Messiah *the Word of God*. So the Chaldee paraphrase frequently calls the Messiah [MIDBAR] (i.e. *the Word*). Now the Messiah being commonly styled the Word of God, the apostle speaking of Him gives Him that name. He may be so called, (1) in respect of the *eternal generation* of his person. The Son of God is essential, internal, and eternal Word of the Father. That as words are the birth of the mind; so is the Son of God eternally begotten by the infinite understanding of the Father reflecting upon His own glory before the world began. (2) In respect of his *office*. As words discover what men will and desire; so it is the office of Christ to discover the will of the Father. The Word of God is that which reveals His will to the children of men. This is true of Christ. (3.) He is the great *promise*. The promise is called "the Word" in Scripture. Now Christ was the first and great promise. The patriarchs of old did long for nothing so much as the fulfilling of that *word* or *promise*, that the Messiah should come into the world and redeem His people. Among men, *word* is often used for *promise*. As when we say, I will give you my word, and I will make good my word, (i.e. *promise*).

In these respects then is Christ styled "the Word."

2. We have the nature *assumed*, noted by that of *flesh*, whereby the whole *human* nature of Christ is signified. Man is by a synecdoche[37] called *flesh* in the Scripture (Ps. 56:4). So is the human nature of Christ elsewhere expressed (John 6:51; 1 Tim. 3:16).

---

[37] A figure of speech in which a part is made to represent the whole.

3. The union of the two natures of Christ is here noted by that of the Word's being made flesh. It is not only the Word was flesh but that He was made so [*Egeneto*] (i.e. He took the nature into personal union with Himself). So these words are declarative of two great mysteries of the gospel. Namely, the incarnation of the Son of God, and the personal union between His two natures.[38]

## Jesus Christ the Son of God, is man as well as God

In the doctrinal handling of this great truth, two things may be enquired into. (1) How it does appear that the Son of God became *man*. (2) The reason why He did so. *How does it appear that the Son of God is man, and not God only?*

## The Scripture expressly & abundantly bears witness to this truth

Christ is expressly called the MAN Christ Jesus (1 Tim. 2:5). He said to the Jews, "you seek to kill a man that has told you the truth" (John 8:40). And He is styled the "Son of Man" (Matt. 16:13). He is set forth by that name about forty times in the New Testament. And He is said to be the "Son of David" (Matt. 1:1), and the Son of the virgin Mary. Christ as God had no mother. As man He was without father, as God without mother. Inasmuch therefore, as the virgin Mary is said to be his mother, He is man as well as God. And the Scripture says that He was born of a woman (Gal. 4:4). And He is called the "seed

---

[38] Athanasius, *On the Incarnation* (Grand Rapids: Christian Classics Ethereal Library); John Calvin, *Institutes of the Christian Religion* (Peabody: Hendrickson, 2015), 297–308; John Owen, *The Glory of Christ* (Edinburgh: Banner of Truth, 2012), 38–49; Mark Jones, *Knowing Christ* (Edinburgh: Banner of Truth, 2016), 25–34.

of the woman" (Gen. 3:15). And He is called by the name of Adam; He is the "last Adam" (1 Cor. 15:45). And it is said, "the second man was the Lord from heaven" (verse 47). Therefore, He is as truly man as the first Adam was. The Scriptures affirm of Him that He became flesh. Without controversy, "great is the mystery of Godliness, God manifest in the flesh" (1 Tim. 3:16). Christ is God incarnate. When the eternal Son of God did assume the human nature, then was God manifest in the flesh.

**The essential parts of a man are affirmed of Christ. Therefore, it is most true that He has a human nature belonging to Him**

A man does consist of two essential parts, namely, a *human body*, and a *rational soul*; both which do belong to Christ. He has a human body; "we are sanctified by the offering of the body of Jesus Christ" (Heb. 10:10). "His own self bore our sins in His own body on the tree" (1 Pet. 2:24). "When Christ had blessed the bread at the Lord's Supper, He broke it and said this is my body" (Matt. 26:26). The members of a human body belong to Him, hence we read of His eyes (John 17:1), and of His hands and His feet (Ps. 22:16). And that too after His resurrection, because Jesus Christ has hands and feet now in his state of exaltation. He has his human nature still, and will have so to all eternity; which human nature of His shall be seen by every eye at the last day (Luke 23:39–40, Rev. 1:7). And He has a rational soul, which is the other essential part of human nature. "His soul was made an offering for sin" (Isa. 53:10). He complained that His soul "was sorrowful unto death" (Matt. 26:38). And when He was dying He said, "Father, into your hands I commend my spirit" (Luke 23:46). The proper faculties of a reasonable soul are ascribed unto Christ (e.g. that of understanding). When He was about 12 years old, He did so reason with the learned doctors, as all that heard Him were astonished at His understanding and "He increased in wisdom" (Luke 2:46, 52). Another faculty of the soul is that of the will; which is also affirmed of Christ: "not my will but yours be done" (Luke 22:42).

**Human actions are affirmed of Christ**
For example: natural and common actions performed by men in common with other creatures such as eating and drinking; these actions did Christ do when in this lower world (Luke 22:15-16, 18). To sit and stand, and walk from place to place, are things not to be affirmed of the divine nature in propriety of speech; because that is infinite and always in all places. But Christ "went up and down doing good" (Acts 10:38). And we read in the Scripture of His sitting and of His walking, and once of His riding to Jerusalem. Moreover, to speak and teach and write, are actions proper to men; and these things did Christ do (Luke 4:15-16, John 8:6-8).

**Human (sinless) infirmities are affirmed of Christ**
Therefore, He is man as well as God. Indeed, as for those sinful infirmities which we are so miserably subject unto, Christ had none of them; but other infirmities He once had. "We have not a high priest who cannot be touched with the feeling of our infirmities, but was in all points tempted like as we are, yet without sin" (Heb. 4:15). It is therefore also said that "God sent His own Son in the likeness of sinful flesh" (Rom. 8:4). The Son of God is not only in the likeness of flesh, for He is made

real flesh, but only like sinful flesh. As the brazen serpent was like a serpent but had no poison in it; so Christ was like unto sinful flesh but never had the least degree of sin in His holy nature. Only as to other infirmities He was as all other men are. It is true that there are many personal infirmities of men which Christ did not experience. There are many diseases which particular persons are afflicted with that Christ was never subject to, but the general infirmities of human nature He did subject unto, namely, to hunger, thirst, weariness, etc. which are the general infirmities of our nature. And so it was with Christ when in this world (Matt. 4:2). Indeed, now that He is entered into His glory, He is not subject to any infirmity; but during His state of humiliation He was so. Hence that state is expressed by the "days of his flesh" (Heb. 5:7) (i.e. the time when He was subject to human sinless infirmities), and Christ has not laid aside the essential properties of His human nature. Though such infirmities as were accidental thereunto and necessary for His state of humiliation are not consistent with His glorified estate; yet He carried to the right hand of God in Heaven His human nature, even a soul and body, the very same that once suffered for the sins of His people. He has flesh and bones, (glorified flesh) now in heaven; and therefore, a glorious body; for so does the Scripture declare and teach us to believe. We have a Savior in heaven, "who shall change our vile bodies that they be fashioned like unto His glorious body" (Phil. 3:21).

We may for the further confirmation of this truth.

**Take notice how it has been mysteriously signified**
In the days of the Old Testament, the Son of God did sometimes appear in the form of a man to the patriarchs; so He did to Abraham; and so to Jacob, and to Joshua, and others (and

some think that He appeared in the likeness that He was to take). We do not read that God the Father or that God the Holy Ghost did ever appear in a human shape to the fathers, only God the Son did so; thereby to signify His future incarnation; that in due time He would really be, as then He seemed to be.

Moreover, the tabernacle was a type of Christ's human nature, which is therefore called "the true Tabernacle which the Lord had pitched and not man" (Heb. 8:2). For the human nature of Christ came not into the world by means of any man but was conceived by the power of the Holy Ghost, and is therefore said to be "the great and perfect tabernacle" (Heb. 8:2; 9:11). And when John prophesies in the Revelation 13:6 that the time should come when men would "blaspheme God's tabernacle," he does foretell the gross idolatry of the Papists in their mass, and their blasphemous doctrine about transubstantiation, by which the highest abuses that can be, are offered to the human nature of Christ in which nature God dwells. In my text it was said "the Word was made flesh," and the next words are, "and dwelt among us." The Greek word is [*eskenose*] which the ancients are wont to interpret [*skenos anelaben*] (i.e. *corpus assumpsit*: He tabernacled among us). The feast of tabernacles did typify the incarnation of Christ, whence the Jews suppose that Christ will be born at the time when that feast is by them observed; and they deride Christians for keeping the feast of Christ's nativity in the tenth month of the year, saying that they place the birth of Christ in the month, wherein they ought rather to place His conception. However, the feast of tabernacles which the children of Israel kept in the seventh month, did signify that God would appear and dwell in our nature. The temple was also a type of Christ's body (John 2:19). Jesus said, "destroy this temple" (probably Christ did with his hand point at His own body as He spoke these words). In verse 21 it is said, "He spoke of the temple of his body." The temple was the most costly, excellent, glorious, house in the world; thereby figuring the human nature of Christ, which was adorned with graces and spiritual excellencies beyond any other man or creature. Particularly, the *veil* of the temple typified the human nature of Christ. "He has consecrated a new (Christ was then newly slain, and there is no other way after this, and therefore, it is still and always new) and living way for us, through the veil, that is to say his flesh" (Heb. 10:20). As there was no entering into the holy of holies but by the veil; so there is no entering into heaven but through that sacrifice of the flesh, (i.e. the human nature of Christ). And this truth is still mysteriously signified by that ordinance of the Lord's Supper. The bread signifies the body and the wine the blood of Christ. And that sacramental action of taking the bread in order to the consecration thereof, puts us in mind of Christ's taking our nature. That is a meditation which should be in our hearts as we see the minister take the bread in order to the blessing and breaking of it. We should then think of Christ's incarnation, that the Son of God has assumed our nature, so that he might die for our sakes.

We come therefore, to enquire into the *reasons* of the doctrine.

Reason 1. *The Word was made flesh, because it was the will of the Father to have it so.* We have formerly treated of the covenant of redemption, and then was showed that this was one article in that covenant, that the Son of God should take unto Him the nature of man. The Father said to Him, "if you will be a redeemer for sinful man, you must yourself become a man, and in that nature do what concerns a redeemer to perform." In compliance with this will of the Father, "the Son of God was manifest in the flesh" (Heb. 10:5, 7; John 14).

Reason 2. *So that He might be a fit mediator between God and the children of men.* "There is one mediator between God and men, the man Christ Jesus" (1 Tim. 2:5). Hence Christ was fit to be a daysman[39] (as Job speaks) between them both. It was altogether necessary that the mediator should be God-man. If Christ had been man *only* He could not have been a mediator; He could not have saved one sinner, nor satisfied for one sin. And if He had not been a man, but God only, He could not have been a mediator. "He that sanctifies and they that are sanctified, are all one" (i.e. of one and the same nature) (Heb. 2:11). Since the elect are partakers of flesh and blood, He Himself took part of the same. Otherwise He could not have died nor have made reconciliation for the sins of His people. Except He had been made flesh, He could not have shed His blood to make atonement for sinners.

Use 1. *We must conclude that ignorance or error about this great truth; is of dangerous consequence to the souls of men.* It is indeed a fundamental article in our Christian faith, the knowledge whereof is necessary to salvation. It is strange to consider that any who live under the gospel should be ignorant of such a plain, easy, common principle of religion; nevertheless, there are such. I have discoursed with some that go under the name of Christians that yet could not tell whether Christ were God or man, but when asked the question, have replied

---

[39] A mediator.

that he was only God, as supposing that a man could not save them. But such dark and horrid ignorance will be destructive to the souls of men. There are those also, who though they do in words acknowledge it to be a great truth that the Son of God became a man; nevertheless, they hold such errors as are not well consistent with the truth which they profess. So do they who maintain the real presence of the body of Christ in the sacrament; which is to say that Christ's body has not the true nature of a body, and in effect to say, that He has only a divine nature. He that takes away the properties of an human nature denies that nature. And if Christ has no other nature but that which is in all places, then He has only a divine nature. There are also a sort of men in the world who hold that there is no Christ but what is within; and that salvation is to be had, not from a Christ without, but from at Christ within. My brethren, take heed of such errors. They that maintain them, let them pretend what they will, they deny the humanity of Christ, and so overthrow the faith and subvert the souls of them that shall be so miserable as to give any credit to their strong delusions.

Use 2. *Hence may we be humbly familiar with the Lord Jesus, and with God through Him.* Indeed, we must carry ourselves humbly and reverently before Him, because He is God as well as man, yet may we be familiar with Him, because He is man as well as God. He is become our near kinsman. Under the law, He that had right to redeem was a near kinsman; so the Son of God, the redeemer of souls, is become our near kinsman. As Boaz told Ruth he was to her, Christ is not ashamed to call us brethren; as being in our nature, a man as we are, though not a sinner as we are (Heb. 2:11). And therefore, He bids believers come and be familiar with Him, and that the terror of His infinite majesty should not make them afraid. When Joseph's brethren being conscious to themselves of their own great guiltiness were afraid and troubled at his presence, he said to them, "come near to me I pray you, I am Joseph your brother" (Gen. 45:4). When believers have a humble sense of their sin and guilt, the Son of God says to them, "come near to me, I am Jesus your Brother. I will make your peace with my Father, and therefore, be not discouraged." Hence Christ causes believers to sit down with Him at His own table. If a great man invites those to his table who are much his inferiors, though he expects that they should know their distances, yet he allows of freedom and familiarity in their communion. And the Son of God who is made man does therefore invite us to His blessed table, because He would have us humbly familiar with Him, Yes, and with God through Christ. Without Christ we may not draw near to that God who is a consuming fire. But having such a one as Jesus the Son of God to lead us by the hand into the presence of the Father of Glory, we may come boldly to the throne of grace. We have boldness of access through Him (Eph. 3:12).

Use 3. *Oh Love Jesus Christ*! Believers have infinite cause to love Him. Should there not be love between kindred and near relations? Christ is our *kinsman* (as but now was shown) our *elder brother*, our *father*, our *husband*. And He is an object worthy to be loved. "He is altogether lovely" (Song. 5:16). If you can set your heart upon a more amiable object, or a lovelier person, never think of loving Him more. But that cannot be. And He deserves all our love, by what He has done for us. He has loved us, and that with an everlasting love. Before the world began He took pleasure in thinking of us, and in the communion which He should forever enjoy with His redeemed ones. Wherefore He says, "I was from everlasting, rejoicing in the habitable part of the earth, and my delights were with the sons of men" (Prov. 8:23, 31). And therefore was He willing to be made flesh. His love moved Him to that infinite condescension. That the blessed Son of God who humbles Himself to behold the things in heaven should condescend to assume our nature into personal union, that He should be willing to be clothed with flesh!

What wonderful love was that! And He does continue to love his saints throughout the days of eternity. "Having loved His own which were in the world, He loved them to the end" (John 13:1). That fire of love which is in the heart of the Son of God towards believers, it was kindled before the world began, and will burn to all eternity. The choicest blessings that ever we did, or shall, or can partake of, we are beholding to Jesus Christ the Son of God for them all. It is in Christ that God does bless us with all "spiritual blessings" (Eph. 1:3). And if it had not been for Christ, we had never had any spiritual blessing. He is our righteousness, He is our life, He is our all. Oh, then let us love Him. Never anyone did for us as Christ has done. Nay, no one in heaven or earth would or could have done so much for us as Christ has done. He died for us and suffered the most bitter death that ever was known. Ignatius was wont to say, "my love is crucified."[40] Christ has been crucified to save us

---

[40]The full quote is as follows: "*And my love is crucified, and there is no fire in me for another love. I do not desire the food of corruption, neither the lusts of this world. I seek the bread of God, which is the flesh of Jesus Christ; and I seek His blood, a drink which is love incorruptible*" —

from being broken forever in the place of dragons, and that we might not be covered with the shadow of eternal death! And shall we not love Him! We cannot exceed bounds in our love to Christ as we may in our love to the world and the things thereof; which indeed is the cause of all the misery we are subject unto. It is all because we love other things so much, and Christ so little. The more we delight in Christ, the more will God delight in us. "The Father Himself loved you, because you have loved me, and have believed that I came out from God" (John 16:27). Therefore, let us love the Son of God, who has loved us, and assumed our nature, and in that nature died and gave Himself for us.

---

Ignatius, *Epistle to the Ephesians*: A. Cleveland Coxe, *Ante-Nicene Fathers. Vol. 1: The Apostolic Fathers, with Justin Martyr, Irenaeus* ed. Alexander Roberts and James Donaldson (New York: Christian Literature Company, 1885), 104.

# 5
# THERE IS A PERSONAL UNION BETWEEN THE TWO NATURES OF CHRIST

The Scriptures make known this wonderful mystery unto us. Wherefore it is said of Christ, "that in Him dwells all the fullness of the Godhead bodily" (Col. 2:9), because He is God and man in one person. He is God manifested in the flesh (1 Tim. 3:16). So that the same person who is God, is also flesh.

For the further opening and confirmation of this doctrine, we shall (1.) Lay down some propositions for the clearing of the truth, and (2) enquire into the reasons of it.

**The personal union of Christ's two natures is that whereby the second person in the Godhead has assumed the individual human nature of Christ to subsist inseparably in the same person**[41]
In this description we have:

1. *The assumer. Namely, the second person of the Godhead who is here called the Word:* "There are three that bear record in heaven, the Father, the Word and the Holy Ghost, and these

---

[41] John Calvin, *Institutes of the Christian Religion* (Peabody: Hendrickson, 2015), 309–316; Herman Bavinck, *Reformed Dogmatics, Vol. 3: Sin and Salvation in Christ* (Grand Rapids: Baker Academic, 2006), 298–308; Matthew Barrett, *Reformation Theology: Robert Letham, Chapter 9: The Person of Christ* (Wheaton: Crossway, 2017), 331–345.

three are one" (1 John 5:7). It is only the Word, or Son of God, and not the Father or the Holy Ghost that is made flesh. It is true that every person in the Godhead has a hand in the incarnation of Christ. God the Father had so who is said to "prepare a body for His Son" (Luke 2:30-31, Heb. 10:5). And God the Holy Ghost had a hand in framing the human nature of Christ. "The birth of Jesus Christ was as follows: when His mother Mary was espoused to Joseph, before they came together she was found with child of the Holy Ghost" (Matt. 1:18). And this was according to what the angel had spoken, who said unto her, "the Holy Ghost shall come upon you, and the power of the Highest shall over shadow you; therefore, also that holy thing that shall be born of you, shall be called the Son of God" (Luke 1:35). But only the second person of the Godhead can be said to assume or to be united to the human nature. As when three persons join together in making a garment and only one puts it on; everyone has a hand in the efficiency of the garment, yet but one wears it. So it is in the efficiency of the human nature of Christ. All the persons in the sacred Trinity did concur, yet it is only the *Word* or *Son* of God that takes that nature into personal union. It is only the second person of the Godhead, and not the Godhead that does immediately assume; for then every person in the Godhead should assume human nature which we may not affirm. It is Sabellianism[42] and heresy to maintain that the Father and the Holy Ghost are incarnate as well as the Son.

---

[42] An ancient heresy developed by Sabellius in the 3rd century AD. This heresy emphasizes the oneness of God and insists that there are not three distinct persons in the Godhead but rather God manifests Himself in three distinct modes (i.e. modalism).

2. *The thing assumed.* Namely, *the singular human nature of Christ.* The Son of God has taken human nature into His own bosom; into nearest union with His own person. Hence He is said to assume flesh (i.e. human nature) and none other, "forasmuch as the children are partaken of flesh and blood, He also Himself took part of the same; for verily He took not on Him the nature of angels, but He took on Him the seed of Abraham" (Heb. 2:14, 16). And this may be affirmed only of the individual human nature of Christ. It cannot without blasphemy and heresy be affirmed of the individual human nature of Abraham or Peter or David or John, or any particular saint that they are personally united to the Son of God. He has taken them into mystical union with Himself, but not into personal union; for that is the royal prerogative of Jesus Christ. Nor indeed was it proper so that great a dignity should be common. As divines rightly observe, "it becomes not the great God, who is one in nature, to communicate his dignity but to one."

3. In this description of the personal union, we have expressed the manner of the subsisting of the human nature thus united to the divine nature of the Son of God. (1.) It does subsist in the same person. (2.) Inseparably.

(1) *In the same Person.* For the human nature of Jesus Christ is not a person itself alone. It is a mystery which all men had been ignorant of had it not been for the human nature of Christ, that it is possible for human nature to subsist without its personality. All other human natures are distinct persons of themselves, but the human nature of Christ is not so. For then there would be *four* persons in the Godhead; *three* of them eternal, and *one* of them made of a woman in the fullness of time.

We must therefore know, that there is in Christ, a personal union, but not a union of *persons*; and a union of *natures*, yet not a union of *persons*. The human nature of Christ did not subsist one moment, before its being united to the Son of God, the second person in the Trinity.

(2) *The human nature of Christ does subsist inseparably as well as personally with the Son of God.* This union is an everlasting union. The human nature never did exist one moment before its being united to the divine, nor ever shall be disunited from it. As long as God shall be God, so long shall the personal union of Christ's human nature with the divine continue. When Christ died and His soul was separated from his body, yet His human nature was not separated from His divine; but when His body lay in the grave and His soul in paradise, both body and soul were united to the divine nature. As death dissolves not the mystical union which is between Christ and the believer, so neither did it the personal union between the two natures of Christ. Hence Christ's incarnation is not properly any part of His humiliation. For His state of humiliation is laid down, whereas His human nature is not laid aside, nor ever shall be.

## By reason of the union of the two natures of Christ: there is a communication of properties

This follows undeniably from the *hypostatical union* of the two natures of Christ, and is also a demonstration of the truth of this doctrine that there is a personal union. Hence that which does belong properly to the person of Christ, is ascribed to either nature (e.g. mediation with the Father belongs to the person of Christ); nevertheless it is ascribed to the manhood. It is said, "the man Christ Jesus is the Mediator" (1 Tim. 2:5). Yet

Christ is not mediator as man only, but as Godman. Likewise, that which does belong to either nature is affirmed of the person. *Eternity*, and *immutability* are essential properties of the divine nature. And yet these properties are affirmed of the person of Christ. "Jesus Christ is the same yesterday, today and forever" (Heb. 13:8). Again, mortality or subjection to death was proper to the human nature, "the bread that I will give is my flesh, which I will give for the life of the world" (John 6:51). It was only the flesh of Christ that died. Yet this is spoken of his person: "God spared not his own son... It is Christ that died" (Rom. 8:32, 34). Hence the Scripture speaks of God's suffering and dying. "God bought the Church with his own blood" (Acts 20:28). "Hereby perceive we the love of God, because He laid down his life" (1 John 3:16). The personal union is the reason of such expressions. For because of that the blood of Christ is truly said to be the blood of God; and the life of Christ to be the life of God. That person who is God, laid down his life and shed His blood to save sinners. Were not the human nature of Christ one in person with the divine nature, it could not be said that God laid down his life.

## The two natures of Christ remain really distinct from one another

It was the heresy of Eutyches[43] that he did confound the two natures of Christ. And there are millions of men in the world at

---

[43] Eutyches was a monk in Constantinople who vehemently opposed Nestorius at the First Council of Ephesus (Nestorianism denies the hypostatic union). He strayed to the opposite end of the spectrum though and was himself declared a heretic at the Council of Chalcedon for his view that the human nature and the divine nature were *fused* together into one single and unique nature. For more in-

this day, who call themselves Christians that are infected with that error. But we must know, that though there be a union, yet there is no confusion of the natures of Christ. And although there be (as has been showed) a communication of properties by reason of the personal union, nevertheless the natures of Christ remain distinct in their properties. Christ has two understandings, a divine understanding which is infinite; in respect whereof He knows all things; yes, what grace is in the hearts of men (John 21:17), and a human understanding which is not omniscient; (though now in glory Christ's understanding as man is enlarged so as to be next to infinite) (Mark 13:42). Hence Christ in respect of His human understanding, He was said to grow in wisdom (Luke 2:52). As man, He knows more now in heaven, than He did when on earth (Rev. 1:1). He has two wills, really distinct (though not contradictory) the one from the other (Luke 22:42). Hence that may be affirmed of one of Christ's natures which cannot be affirmed of the other. For example, it may be said of the human nature of Christ, that it was, conceived, born, crucified, buried, ascended into glory; none of which things can be said of the divine nature. Of the human nature of Christ we may say, there was a time when it was not (Gal. 4:4). Time began when the world began, and the world was near four thousand years old before the human nature of Christ was made. But we cannot say of the divine nature of Christ, that once it was not. "In the beginning was the Word, and the Word was with God, and the Word was God" (John 1:1). We may now say of the human nature of Christ that the heavens do contain it, and shall do so till the time of restitution

---

formation on this subject, see Philip Schaff's work *Creeds of Christendom, Volume 1*, 6th Ed. (New York: Harper & Brothers, 1931), 52-53, 56, 61, 102-103, 236, 305, 334, 337, & 416.

of all things. But as for His divine nature, the heaven of heavens cannot contain it. We may say and must believe, concerning the divine nature of Christ that it is omnipresent: "where two or three are gathered together in my name, there am I in the midst of them" (Matt. 18:20). But we cannot say so of the human nature; for that were to make finite infinite, and in effect to say, that Christ has only a divine, and not a human nature. It were to say, that the Word is not made flesh.

## The assumption of the human nature has caused no real change in the person of the Son of God

Though the Word was made flesh, there was no real change wrought in him thereby; only a new respect, a new relation. That person which before was only God, is now man as well as God. As a man that is clothed is the same as he was before he put on his clothing; so the Son of God is the same as He was before He put on human nature. Indeed, the human nature is changed, being meliorated[44] and gloriously advanced by this assumption into personal union with the divine nature, but the Son is the same. He is an unchangeable person (Heb. 1:8, 12). As when God created the world there was no change in God, but in the creature only, so it is here.

## This personal union is a great mystery

The whole doctrine of Christ is mysterious: "You may understand my knowledge in the mystery of Christ" (Eph. 3:4). So in special, the doctrine of Christ's person and of the union of His two natures, is very mysterious. That which is not known but by divine supernatural revelation is called a mystery in

---

[44] Made better, improved.

Scripture. Now all our knowledge in this personal union, is from the gospel. If men have only the light of nature and the book of the creature to inform them, they will never know anything of this glorious mystery. It is a wonderful union.

There are three unions spoken of in the Scripture which are wonderful. (1) The mystical union which is between Christ and the believer, which was mysteriously signified by Eve's being taken out of Adam's side, and then being married to him by the Lord Himself, as the apostle shows (Eph. 5:30-32). (2) The union of diverse persons in one nature; The Father, Son, and Spirit, though three distinct persons, have but one name or nature (Matt. 28:20). They are three witnesses, and therefore three persons; yet but one in respect of nature and of being (1 John 6:7). The mystery of the trinity is a wonderful mystery. (3) The union of diverse natures in one person; which is that we are speaking of. This is not only a mystery, but a great mystery. It must needs be confessed, that "Great is the mystery of religion, God manifest in the flesh" (1 Tim. 3:16). The holy angels bow down their heads to search into this mystery, which will be the wonderment of saints and angels, throughout the days of eternity (1 Pet. 1:12).

Hence the Devil has set himself to oppose and darken those truths which concern the person of Christ. Most of the heresies whereby Satan has troubled the Church, have proceeded from ignorance in the mystery about Christ's person. Either by dividing his person which is but one (as the Nestorians, who make two persons of Christ) or by confounding his natures, which are two, or by denying one of his natures. Therefore, it is most necessary, that we should have a distinct and clear knowledge about this, since it is a great mystery. Ignorance here, error here, may prove destructive to the souls of men.

Question: *But, for what reasons did the Son of God assume human nature into personal union with Himself?*

Answer 1. *So that the sufferings of that nature might become infinitely meritorious.* The death and blood of all the men in the world, would not satisfy for one sin, nor redeem one sinner. Will the Lord be pleased with "thousands of rams, or ten thousands of rivers of oil? If they give the fruit of their body for the sin of their soul, will that appease him?" (Mic. 6:7). No verily, it was then necessary that Christ should be both God and man in one person. The value of the obedience of Christ is augmented and aggravated from the dignity of his person. The obedience of an infinite person is of infinite worth and value. Now, though the human nature of Christ which suffered is not infinite, yet the person to which that nature belongs, is so. Hence, For Christ to die, is more than if all the men on earth, and all the angels in heaven had died; for they are not God, but Christ is so.

Answer 2. *The Son of God did assume human nature, that Satan might be so much the more crushed and confounded.* "For this purpose the Son of God was manifested, that He might destroy the works of the Devil" (1 John 3:8). It was man that Satan envied and murdered from the beginning. Therefore, God would punish his malice by crushing his head with that very nature which he had envied and sought the destruction of. God delights to meet with sinners by suitable punishments, and so to make that sin most heavy, which was at first most delightful.

Satan rejoiced to think that he had destroyed human nature, but therefore God would meet with him for it, and make that very nature light heavy upon him which he hoped and endeavored to destroy.

Answer 3. *The Word became flesh, so that He might the better sympathize with His people in all their afflictions and temptations* (Heb. 2:17; 4:15). Yes, therefore, the Son of God did not only assume our nature, but became subject to the sinless infirmities thereof (Heb. 5:2). It had not been possible for Him to have had such a sympathizing with His people as now He has, if He had not partaken of the same nature.

## Hence Jesus Christ is the great wonder of the world

Jesus Christ is a none-such.[45] There is no such person in heaven or earth concerning whom it may be said, That person is both God and man, excepting only the man Christ Jesus. Men are apt to be taken with wonders as the King of Babylon sent to Hezekiah to enquire of the wonder. Here is a wonder for us all to be taken with: that the Word should be made flesh. If we do a little meditate on the incarnation and the personal union of the two natures of Christ, we shall see that which is wonderful. What a wonder it is, that two natures so infinitely distant should meet together in one person. The divine nature is infinitely above the most glorious creatures. "God humbles Himself to behold the things that are done in heaven" (Ps. 113:5–6). And the human nature, what a poor thing is it in itself considered! One may even wonder that God should so much as

---

[45] A person regarded as excellent or perfect; a person without equal.

look upon man. "What is man that you are mindful of him, or the son of man that you visit him! (Ps. 8:4).

But, that God should become one with man, yes, that God should become a man, that the Word should be made flesh, how wonderful it is! In former times, the saints have been afraid to behold the glory of God sparkling in the countenance of an angel, but behold and wonder: here is a human nature not only seeing the glory of God, but united to Him. An Immanuel, God dwelling in our nature. That majesty and meanness should thus meet together! Is it not a wonder, that one and the same person should be capable of a double generation, one eternal, and the other in time? But this is true concerning Jesus Christ. He is the eternally begotten Son of God. It is a generation which neither had a beginning or ending (Ps. 2:7). Yet He was brought forth in the "fullness of time," in respect of His being made flesh (Gal. 4:4). Is it not a wonder that a man should be his own mother's maker and father? Yet this may we affirm of Christ. The virgin Mary was His own mother, in respect of His being made flesh; yet He was her father in respect of creation by the power of His divine nature. The Son of God made her of whom it is said, He Himself was made. He is styled the "everlasting Father" (Is. 9:6). He is the father of all believers who are called His seed; and therefore, He is His mother's father. And is it not a wonder that a woman should be the mother of God! Yes, a poor, mortal, sinful woman; yet because of the personal union of the two natures of Christ, this is true. The virgin Mary was, though a very holy woman, yet not without sin. Did not Christ die to save her? And who did He die for but only for sinners? Yet she was the mother of the Son of God. Therefore Elizabeth said, "Whence is this, that the mother of my Lord should come unto me!" (Luke 1:43). So then, Christ is the most wonderful person, His name shall be called wonderful.

## The human nature of Christ must necessarily be most pure & sinless altogether[46]

Adam was innocent at his first creation. He had no sin as he came out of God's hands. Yet there was a possibility of his sinning; but it was impossible that the nature of Christ should become sinful; that being inconsistent with the grace of personal union. This nature was united to the Godhead, from the first moment of its conception. Hence the angel said to the virgin Mary, "The Holy Ghost shall come upon you and the power of the Highest shall overshadow you; therefore, also that holy thing that shall be born of you, shall be called the Son of God" (Luke 1:35). So He was free from original sin, that corruption of nature which has infected all mankind besides. For Adam stood in the capacity of a public person on the behalf of such only as should come into the world by generation, which Christ did not; but by miraculous conception from the Holy Ghost, nor did he ever become guilty of actual sin. Though He lived in the world thirty-two years, He never spoke one sinful word, not ever had one sinful thought in His heart all that while. He kept the whole law perfectly, so as never to fail in so much as one particular. There never was any other man that did so, or that could do so since Adam sinned. He is, and always was altogether lovely.

---

[46] Mark Jones, *Knowing Christ* (Edinburgh: Banner of Truth, 2016), 101–108.

**Human nature is dignified above any created nature**
For the Word has not assumed any other nature but that. It is true that of all created natures, the angelical is the most excellent and glorious. Angels are better than men simply considered (Ps. 8:5). Yet in respect of the Word's being made flesh the human nature is exalted above the angelical. The Son of God is made a man, but He is not made an angel. By reason of this personal union, diverse things may be said of a man, that cannot be affirmed of the most glorious angel in heaven (e.g. It may be said of a man, that he is God as well as man). The soul of that man is the soul of God, and the body of that man is the body of God (1 Cor. 11:24). It may be said of Him that is a man, that He is (though not a man) equal with God. It cannot be said of any one among all the angels in heaven, that he is equal with God. It may be said of one among the sons of men, that he is "fellow to the Lord of Hosts" (Zech. 13:7), and "equal with God" (John 5:18). "Christ counted it no robbery to say, that He was equal with God" (Phil. 2:6). If any angel in heaven should say that he is equal with God, it would be the highest robbery, the most sacrilegious impiety so to rob God of His glory. There is none among the sons of the mighty that may be compared with Him. Again, it may be said of Him who is a man, that He did create the world. Though the world was created thousands of years before He became a man; nevertheless it is a truth, that He who is now a man, did create heaven and earth. A saint in glory may point unto the man Christ Jesus and say, "that man there made all the creatures in the world." "All things were made by Him, and without Him was not anything made that was made" (John 1:3). This is more than can be affirmed of any angel or archangel. Once more, "a man shall be the judge of all the earth" (Acts 17:31). God has appointed a

day "in the which He will judge the world in righteousness, by the man whom He has ordained" (Acts 17:31). This cannot be affirmed of any angel. The world to come is not put in subjection to the angels. Therefore, human nature is advanced above angelical nature, and so above all created nature. As the Jews were advanced above all nations in respect of Christ's being of them; (Rom. 9:5) so indeed, men are respected above all creatures, in that the Son of God is become a man, not having assumed any other nature but this into personal union with Himself.

**Hence: to abuse human nature, especially the human nature of Christ, is a very great evil**

The Son of God has dignified human nature, and therefore, for any to abuse or abase it is a horrid thing. This shows us how great an evil it is to wrong any man. Though he be the meanest man in the world, yet he was made after the image of God. And the eternally blessed Son of God has taken the same nature into personal union. Therefore, to wrong any man in his soul or in his body, is great iniquity. Especially when men abuse and abase themselves, when they make their own natures vile by sins there is no small evil in what they do. In a peculiar manner, sins against the body vilify the nature of man. The apostle aggravates the sin of uncleanness from that consideration (1 Cor. 6:15, 18).

And this is a suitable meditation to be in the heart at the Lord's Table; to think, Christ has dignified human nature so as to take it into personal union with Himself! Then let me not abuse that nature. Is the Word become flesh? Then let not me abuse that flesh by any vile lusts. I say, injuries to human nature have no small evil in them. But above all, abuses offered to the human nature of Christ are an exceeding provocation to God. Hence the wickedness of the Jews in crucifying Christ was so heinous and horrid; and God's wrath is come upon them to the uttermost for it. God has punished them, so as the like never was, nor ever shall be (Matt. 24:21). Surely they must be guilty of some extraordinary wickedness, worse than all the idolatries of their forefathers. For they have been the most miserable nation under heaven for these sixteen hundred years. Never was there a nation so plagued once the world began.

And what is it that they have done worse than their fathers, excepting this one thing of the shedding the precious blood of the Son of God? And hence it is, that coming unworthily to the Lord's Table is such a dreadful evil. "Whosoever shall eat this bread or drink this cup of the Lord unworthily, shall be guilty of the body and blood of the Lord" (1 Cor. 11:27). What, shall men disregard such a body as is personally united to the Son of God! Do we not discern that it is the LORD's body? He that does not is guilty of the blood of the Lord; yes of Him who is the LORD of heaven and earth. To be guilty, of the blood of any man is a sad thing, much more to be guilty of the blood of a worthy person. But what is it then to be guilty of the blood of Him who is the LORD of life and of glory, and who is God and man in one Person!

# 6
# JESUS CHRIST IS THE MEDIATOR

"Jesus Christ is the Mediator."
Hebrews 12:24

The apostle having in the fourteenth verse of this chapter exhorted the believing Hebrews to follow holiness, he does urge that exhortation by an argument taken from the consideration of that better state, which believers under the New Testament are in, compared with those of the Old. More holiness should be the fruit of all gracious dispensations. The more God does for us, the more ought we to do for Him. Now He has done more for New than for Old Testament believers. Therefore, they ought to be more holy in heart and life, and to abound in those fruits of righteousness which are by Christ to the praise and glory of God. That gracious state which believers under the gospel are in, is set forth;

1. *Negatively*, in the 18th-21st verses of this chapter; the scope and sum whereof amounts to this much: we are not now under the sad, severe and servile dispensations of the law, but under one more gracious, and therefore, we ought to be more holy. Holiness was required under the law. When that was promulgated, the children of Israel were to purify themselves, and to wash their clothes; by which ceremonies they were

taught inward holiness. Much more should they to whom the gospel is made known, follow holiness.

2. The happy state of believers is described *affirmatively* in this with the two preceding verses. Wherein is showed that believers now are in a more filial yes and celestial state than formerly. Mount Zion is far more excellent than Mount Sinai. The city of the living God, [is better] than the wilderness. It is better to have to do with the holy angels as fellow servants, than as when the law was given in that dreadful manner by the disposition of angels. The Church of the *Firstborn* is better than the Jewish Synagogue. The manifestation of God as the Judge of all the world, does exceed the manifestation of God as a lawgiver to the Children of Israel only. The saints in heaven are more perfect than they on earth. JESUS is better than Moses. The New Testament [is better] than the Old. The blood of Christ is better than that which is offered by Abel, or by the fathers of old. Even so and therefore, the state of believers under the New Testament, is much more desirable than that of believers under the Old Testament. It is better being a Christian than a Jew; and thence more holiness is required.

From the words considered both in themselves, and as they lie before us in the context, there are especially *three doctrines* observable:

Doctrine 1. *That Jesus Christ is the mediator.*[47]

---

[47] John Owen, *The Glory of* Christ (Edinburgh: Banner of Truth, 2012), 50-62; John Calvin, *Institutes of the Christian Religion* (Peabody: Hendrickson, 2008), 297-303; Herman Bavinck, *Reformed Dogmatics, Vol. 3: Sin and Salvation in Christ* (Grand Rapids: Baker Academic, 2006), 361-364;

Doctrine 2. *That there is a New Testament, whereof Jesus is the mediator.*

Doctrine 3. *That the knowledge and consideration of this truth, that Jesus Christ is the mediator of the New Testament, does oblige Christians to endeavor after a great measure of holiness.*

Only to the first of these doctrines at present, namely, *that Jesus Christ is the mediator.* This great gospel truth may be explained and confirmed in several propositions:

## Sin has made a breach between the blessed God & the children of men

This is evidently implied when it is said, there is a mediator. If Adam had not fallen, and so fallen out with the holy and glorious majesty of heaven, there would have been no need of a mediator. The apostle says, "a mediator, is not of one" (Gal. 3:20). If God and man had continued to be at one, there would have been no mediator. Mediation presupposes a breach. If man had not sinned and so broke with God, the eternal Son of God would not have taken on Him the office of a mediator. Sin has bred a woeful distance and separation between God and the sinner (Is. 59:2). Yes, "sinners are enemies to God" (Rom. 3:7). And this is true concerning all by nature. Every man considered as out of Christ is an enemy and a rebel against heaven and under the disfavor of the Most High. The elect themselves "are by nature the children of wrath even as others" (Eph. 2:3).

## Jesus Christ has, on the behalf of His elect, undertaken to make up the breach

Christ has taken up the controversy between the blessed God and poor sinners and is under engagement to reconcile them. Therefore, He is said to be a mediator. A mediator [*mesites*] is a middleperson who comes between two differing parties to set them at one again. It is noted concerning Moses, when he saw two persons at variance, he would have "set them at one again" (Acts 7:26). He offered to be a mediator between them. He was in that a type of Christ who has not only attempted, but gloriously accomplished a reconciliation between heaven and earth, God and the world. When the first covenant was broken, and thereby God and man set at variance; the question was, who shall make up this breach? The Son of God steps in and undertakes to do it. Therefore, He is said to be the Mediator of the New Covenant. Hence, He is in the Scripture styled the "Prince of Peace" (Is. 9:6). And so to be our peace, (i.e. our peacemaker) (Eph. 2:14), and the reconciler of God to the world, and of the world to God (Col. 1:20; 2 Cor. 9:18–19), He does conciliate (i.e. obtain the favor of God for his people). He causes believers on him to become favorites in the court of heaven. Hence, we often read of the grace of Christ; thereby is meant the favor of God obtained by Christ. But, how does Christ do this?

## Christ is invested with a sacred office

He stands under office-relation. And He is said to be a mediator, not merely in that He is a middle person in the sacred and eternal Trinity, but because He does, by virtue of office-relation, interpose between God and perishing sinners. There are many names and titles given to Christ in the Scripture, whereby His office-relation is signified. This name of a mediator is a name of office. So He is called God's servant, "I will bring forth my servant the branch" (Zech. 3:8). Christ is called a *branch* in respect of His human nature; a *servant* in respect of His office-relation. Hence, He is styled the "Angel of the Covenant," because He is the "mediator of the New Covenant" (Mal. 3:1). Christ is not called an angel in respect of nature, so indeed He is called God, and so He is called *man*, but not an *angel*. He took not on him the nature of angels. Therefore, He is said to be an angel to denote his office. Hence, He is styled an "apostle" (Heb. 3:1), a "bishop" (1. Pet. 2.), a "minister" (Heb. 8:1, 6), a priest, a prophet, and a king (as afterwards may more fully be declared). Now all these names are of *office*. Moreover, those things which are required to constitute an *officer*, are hereby truly affirmed concerning Christ. Three things have been observed as requisites in one that is invested into sacred office.

1. *Qualifications.* God does first fit men for their work before he puts them upon it. He never sent any man upon an errand but gave him legs to go upon. Now thus it is true, concerning the man Christ Jesus. He, (and He only) is wonderfully qualified for the work of mediation which my text speaks of. In the temple (which was a type of Christ) there were utensils for every service required therein. This signifying that Christ, (the true temple), was every way furnished for all that work which as a mediator is incumbent on Him. Hence, He is said to be anointed (Ps. 45:2). The signification of the Hebrew word *Messiah*, and the Greek word, *Christ*, is *anointed*. How? Not materially but spiritually; (i.e. in respect of spiritual qualifications and endowments fitting Him for his work). The gifts of the

Holy Spirit were most plentifully poured on Him (Is. 11:1-3). There never was man or angel, that had such gifts of the Spirit as Christ (considered as man) has. And as to grace and holiness, He is admirably endowed and qualified. He is full of grace, so as that of His fullness we have all received, and that grace for grace: "for God gives the Spirit without measure unto Him" (John 1:14, 16; 3:34).

2. Another thing required to constitute an officer is an *outward call*. Inward qualification without external vocation is not enough to make an officer. No man ought to take that honor to himself except he be called of God, as was Aaron (Heb. 5:4). Ordinary officers have their call from God by man, and extraordinary officers have their call *immediately* from God as the apostle does distinguish (Gal. 1:1). Christ had His call from God, who did (to speak after the manner of men) give Him a commission, as it were under hand and seal, to undertake the work of a redeemer: "for Him has God the Father sealed" (John 6:27). And of Him does God say, "I the Lord have called you in righteousness, and will give you for a covenant to the people" (Is. 42:6). Therefore, He may be well called the *Mediator of the New Covenant*.

3. In order to consummating sacred office relation, *consecration*, and solemn *separation* is necessary. Aaron and his sons were to be consecrated to the Lord, that they might minister in the priest's office (Ex. 30:30). "And the Holy Ghost said, separate me Barnabas and Saul for the work whereunto I have called them" (Acts 13:2). God Himself has consecrated his Son Jesus Christ to the work of a mediator. "The Son is conse-

crated forever more" (Heb. 7:28). "Him the Father has sanctified and sent into the world" (John 10:31). Yes, and Jesus has set Himself apart for the work of a mediator between God and the elect. Therefore He says, "For your sakes I sanctify myself" (John 17:19). There is a sanctification in respect of consecration and separation to the service of God; which glorious mystery is indeed declared in the administration of the Lord's Supper. For when the elements are separated and solemnly consecrated, we are thereby taught that Christ has been set apart as the *Mediator of the New Covenant*. But this will appear further by speaking to the next proposition.

**The Father has committed the work of redemption to the Son of God, who has accordingly undertaken that charge**
(1) I say the Father has committed that work to Christ. God has said to His Son: "as for the work of redemption, I leave that to you; you take care of that matter." Upon this account it is that Christ is said to receive a commandment and charge from God the Father. "As the Father gave me commandment (said Christ when he was going to die for the redemption of his elect) even so do I" (John 14:31). He neither did nor suffered any thing in order to the salvation of His people but what God bid him do. Hence all the work which Christ did in the world, is said to be the work which the "Father gave Him to do" (John 17:4). On this account He is said to be inferior to the Father; not in respect of nature, as He is the Son of God, but as He is the mediator. (John 10:29-30). Yes, He is God's commissioner (to express heavenly mysteries by earthly similitudes). He has the great seal of heaven to authorize Him to act as mediator. Hence, He is called the "Lord's messenger" (Mal. 3:1), and in

John's Gospel, Christ is said to be sent of God, no less than twenty times over.

(2) Jesus Christ has accepted this charge. Though it be the greatest work, and weightiest charge that ever was, yet Christ (who alone was able) has undertaken it. This might serve for a description of Christ's mediatorial office: *it is that charge which He has undertaken in order to the salvation of the elect.* Though He be in respect of nature, equal with God, He took upon Him the form of a *servant*. And being found in fashion as a man, he became obedient unto death. Hence, Christ is styled a *surety*. Jesus is made a surety of a "better Testament" (Heb. 7:22), which implies the same thing with this of His being the Mediator of the New Covenant. God says, "my law must be fulfilled, and my justice must be satisfied." Now Christ the Son of God comes in and says, "as for those things, I will undertake to see them alone." He engages to do that for them, which they are never able to do for themselves. There was a personal debt of perfect obedience unto the law, owing to God. This Christ has performed. Therefore, He put His name into the covenant. "He was made under the law. And that He might be so, He was made of a woman" (Gal. 4:4). So He has discharged believers on Him from being under the law as a covenant. There was also a debt of satisfaction to offended justice, necessary to be discharged. This was such a debt as all the world was never able to pay. Men and angels and all creatures would have proved bankrupts forever had this debt been charged upon them. But Christ who alone could make satisfaction has undertaken it. A learned annotator on Isaiah 53:7 has well observed that that Scripture is a most pregnant place for the satisfaction made by Christ's sufferings for our sins were the text fitly rendered and rightly understood. For their words, "He was oppressed, and

He was afflicted," should be read, "it was exacted, and He answered." You know that *discharging* a debt, is called *answering* it. Thus our debt was *exacted* of Christ our surety, and He *answered*, and so has caused our bond to be canceled that it shall not be put in suit against us (Col. 2:14). Christ says unto God concerning the believer, as sometimes Paul wrote to Philemon concerning Onesimus, "If he has wronged you or owes you ought, put that on my account, I will repay it" (Phil. 1:18). So has He discharged the office of a mediator.

### Jesus Christ as mediator, prophet, priest, & king

The mediatorial office of Christ comes under that three-fold respect, it is prophetical, priestly, kingly. Christ has the wisdom of a prophet, the holiness of a priest, and the power of a king. This threefold office may be particularly hinted at in that Scripture where Christ says, "I am the way, the truth, and the life" (John 14:6). As priest He is the way unto the Father, as prophet He is the truth, as king He is the life. The elect of God, by reason of the fall, are laboring under a three-fold malady and misery, namely, ignorance, alienation from God, and utter inability to help themselves. To the first of these the prophetical office of Christ does *mediate* or bring a remedy, to the second, His priestly, to the third His kingly office is a sovereign help. He is that prophet which the Lord spoke unto Moses saying, "I will raise up a prophet like unto you, and it shall come to pass, that whoever will not hearken unto my words which He shall speak in my name, I will require it of him" (Deut. 18:19). So did the Disciples upon knowledge and much experience testify that "Jesus of Nazareth was a prophet mighty in deed and word before God, and all the people" (Luke 24:19). Now, Christ is said to be a prophet not in respect of nature, but office;

not as God absolutely considered, but as mediator. And God does not reveal His will immediately but mediately by Jesus Christ: "God has in these last days spoken to us by His Son" (Heb. 1:1). "The revelation of Jesus Christ which God gave unto Him to show unto His servants" (Rev. 1:1). Christ as the prophet of His Church has revealed all necessary truth. So the holy Scriptures are from Him. The blessed Bible is the Word of Christ. In special, Christ as the great prophet of His people, has made known the Mystery of the New Covenant.

Likewise, the mediatorial office of Christ is *kingly*. It is most true that there is an eternal, essential sovereignty which belongs to Christ as God coeternal and coequal with the Father, but there is moreover, a *donative*[48] Kingdom which belongs to Him as *mediator* under the Father (Ps. 2:6; Matt. 28:18; John 5:27). God rules over all but by Christ, into whose hands all things are committed by the Father. Therefore, Ezekiel in that glorious vision (1:26), saw a throne and a man upon it, signifying that Christ as man and mediator has the government of the world put into His hands, to dispose of all affairs so as shall be to the glory of the Father, and the good and salvation of His people.

But eminently, Christ is said to be a *mediator* in respect of his *priestly* office. Hence, He is called *Jesus the Mediator*. Why Jesus? Because the great design of the apostle in his Epistle to the Hebrews is to describe the priesthood of Christ. Now, *Jesus* is a name which does respect and note Christ's priestly office. "We have a great high priest that is passed into the Heavens, [JESUS] the Son of God" (Heb. 4:14). The priest under the law, did two things especially:

---

[48] Special Gift.

(1) He did by offering sacrifice "make an atonement for the people" (Lev. 7:7). When God was offended, if the priest did offer sacrifice for the people, He was pacified towards them. Now that was with respect to the sacrifice of Christ. For it was not possible that those other sacrifices should of themselves expiate the guilt of the least sin (Heb. 10:4). Christ then is said to be a mediator inasmuch as he has by the sacrifice of Himself purged away our sins, and obtained our peace with God (Rom. 5:10-11).

(2) The priest offered *incense*. So, Christ has not only made *satisfaction*, but He does make *intercession* (1 John 2:1-2). He is gone to heaven for that end which was typified by the priest's entering into the holy place, there to present incense before the Lord. If the priest should have only offered sacrifice, and not gone into the holy place to offer incense, he would not have done his whole work; so if Christ had not impetrated[49] the mercy of God for sinners by intercession as well as sacrifice, He would not be a perfect priest. Which thing is intended by the apostle, when he says concerning Christ, "If He were on earth he should not be a Priest" (Heb, 8:4). Because should He have continued on earth and not gone to heaven there to intercede for his people, He would have done but half the work of a priest. But thus Christ is a mediator, inasmuch as He does *intercede,* and so *mediate* with the Father on the behalf of those that have sinned.

## Jesus Christ is the only mediator

It is not only true that He is a mediator, but that He *alone* is so. "There is one God, and one Mediator between God and man,

---

[49] Begged for.

the Man Christ Jesus" (1 Tim. 2:5). Wherefore my text does not only say that Jesus is *a* mediator, but that He is *the* mediator of the New Covenant; implying that He, and He only is so. To be a mediator, is a Godlike royalty, and can belong but to one. Indeed, Moses in respect of his standing between the Lord and His people was a typical mediator (Deut. 5:5; Gal. 3:19). But the mediator is here in my text set in opposition to Moses. There neither is, nor ever was, nor ever shall there be, such a mediator as Christ is besides Himself alone. This mysterious and glorious truth of the gospel is evident from several arguments.

1. It was signified by *types* in the days of the Old Testament. "Moses alone was to come near the Lord" (Ex. 24:2). "There might not be any man in the tabernacle of the congregation when the priest went to make atonement" (Lev. 16:17). The high priest went *alone* into the second tabernacle (Heb. 9:7). Moreover, there was to be but one high priest at the same time. By all which things are signified, that there is no mediator to be acknowledged besides Jesus Christ alone.

2. None but Christ is *fit* to be the mediator. No one else in heaven or in earth is both God and man. He is the true Immanuel. He is Immanuel not only in *name*, as Isaiah's son was (being in that respect a type of Christ), but in *deed*. He the *true* God being made man, dwelt with us and among us men. Christ is God manifest in the flesh, and there is no Godman but He. And therefore, none but He was fit to come in as a daysman between the holy God and offending sinners (Job 9:32). There is none else fit to be a mediator of satisfaction besides JESUS. If He had been *God only*, He could not have satisfied divine justice in

a way of suffering. The divine nature cannot suffer. The eternal Godhead cannot die. Had Christ been *man only* His sufferings would not have been satisfactory. They would not have been of sufficient value to compensate for the infinite wrong which has been done to God by the sins of men. For Christ who is God to suffer, though but for a few hours, is more than if all men and angels had weltered under the wrath of God to eternity. Moreover, the weight of the guilt of sin which was imputed to Christ, and the wrath of the Father which lay upon Him, would have crushed Him under the insupportable burden of it had He not been more than a man. So it was necessary that He should be both God and man, that his sufferings might become satisfactory. And this Jesus the Son of God is the fittest to be a mediator of intercession, because He is most dear unto God, He in whom His very soul does delight; the Son of His Love. God's ear is always open to Him. "Father, I thank you that you have heard me, and I know that you hear me always" (John 11:42).

3. That has been required of the *mediator*, which none but *Christ* was ever able to perform. He must become a surety for miserably indebted and undone sinners (Heb. 7:22). He must therefore, in all respects become subject to and fulfill the law. He must satisfy all the righteous demands thereof, both in respect of *active* and *passive* obedience (Gal. 3:13). Meriting salvation was required of Him. Christ's mediatorial obedience is (and it was necessary it should be) *meritorious*. If He could not have *merited* life for sinners, He could not have been a *mediator*. When there is a work done that according to the rules of justice such a reward is due for it: that is merit. No man or angel was ever able to merit heaven at the hands of God, but only the man

Christ Jesus. By these things then it does appear, that He is the *only* mediator.

## Jesus Christ is a mediator on the behalf of all those that belong to the covenant

The elect of God, the Church of the Firstborn, are all concerned in the mediation of Christ. They are the *seed* of Christ, for whom His soul has travailed (Is. 53:11). Hence His mediatorial obedience is said to be for many: "By the obedience of one shall many be made righteous" (Rom. 5:19). The elect of God though but few compared with others, yet in themselves considered they are many. And He is said to be a mediator for all: "In Christ (i.e. in and through Him as mediator of the new covenant) shall all be made alive" (1 Cor. 15:22). All in that Scripture must be understood in a *restrictive* sense (i.e. for all such as are there spoken of): *all that are made alive*. It is in Christ that they are so. He tasted death for *every man*: that is to say, every man among those sons whom Christ will bring to glory, He has tasted death for him (Heb. 2:9-10). He is mediator on behalf of the *world*: yes, of the *whole world* (1 John 2:1), that is, for all the *elect* of God among Gentiles as well as Jews. There is not one elect soul, but Christ is a mediator for that soul; even for as many as the Father has given to Him. He will not suffer so much as one of them to be lost, if His own blood and intercession can (as most certainly it can) save them (John 18:9, and 17:10).

And Christ is a mediator for the elect, not only after they believe (though then in a peculiar manner; if any man that has fellowship with him fall into sin, Jesus Christ the righteous is an advocate with the Father for him) but before they believe Christ has been a mediator on their behalf: "Neither pray I for these alone, but for them also which shall believe on me" (John 17:20). Otherwise they would never believe. Hence it is that the covenant takes hold on *all the house of Israel* (i.e. the *elect of God*). It cannot be but that a new heart should be given to them. They must repent and believe. Christ has died to purchase grace as well as glory for their souls (John 10:18). Nor is Christ a mediator for any else but only the elect of God. He is a mediator of intercession for none else: "I pray not for the world, but for them which you have given me, for they are thine" (John 17:9). We may be sure then that He has not been a mediator of satisfaction for them. If Christ had died for them that perish, then satisfaction is required twice for the same debt. If Christ has undertaken and satisfied for them; why then are they made an eternal sacrifice to the justice of God. We may not think that Christ has died in vain (Gal. 2:21). Yet so it would be if His blood has been shed for those that shall have no benefit by it.

### Jesus Christ is an eternal mediator

There was before the world began an eternal transaction between the Father and the Son concerning the work of redemption, wherein the Father agreed with the Son, that if He would satisfy divine justice, then the elect should be saved; and the Son engaged that he would do it. And in order thereunto would become a man, and "make himself an offering for sin" (Is. 53:10). In this respect He was set up as a mediator from everlasting (Prov. 8:23). Also, the mediation of Christ has taken place in all ages of the world, from the very beginning of it. "He was slain from the foundation of the world" (Rev. 13:8).

He was so typically in respect of those sacrifices which were once of divine institution, and began with the first age of the world, and in respect of the decree of God; also in respect of the efficacy of His death. Indeed, The Son of God actually began the work of a redeemer when He became incarnate, and first entered upon His state of humiliation. But before that God took the word of His Son concerning this matter so that His mediation was effectual before His incarnation. And thence the sins of the elect who died before Christ came into the world were pardoned, as well as those who have been born since that. "He is the mediator of the New Testament, that by means of death, for the redemption of the transgressions that were under the first Testament, they which were called might receive the promise of eternal inheritance" (Heb. 9:15). It is therefore, also said concerning Old Testament believers that, "they without us should not be made perfect" (Heb. 11:11, 40). The meaning of which may be, that they were not brought to heaven and happiness in one way, and we in another; but both we and they are made perfect by the death and mediation of Christ. So that the first believers that ever were in the world, had their sins pardoned and their souls saved by virtue of the merit and mediation of Jesus Christ.

And He will continue to mediate to the end of the world. "He is a priest forever, after the order of Melchizedek" (Ps. 110:1). Whatever Christ does as mediator, is done either in a state of humiliation or exaltation: the first of these is finished. The work designed for His state of humiliation is blessedly accomplished. The other part is His mediation, He is now, being exalted to the right hand of majesty on high, in the actual performance of and will be so as long as this world shall endure. "Wherefore He is able to save to the uttermost them that come unto God by Him, since He ever lives to make intercession for you" (Heb. 7:28). Christ, now that He is in heaven, does present before God the virtue and value of his blood. So is He a mediator before the throne of grace. Hence His blood is said to speak: "We are come to the blood of sprinkling which speaks better things than that of Abel" (Heb. 12:24). There is now before the throne "a Lamb as it had been slain" (Rev. 9:6), And when God looks upon Him, it speaks for mercy, pardon, life, and salvation to be bestowed upon all them for whom the Lamb has been slain. And this Jesus declares it to be His mind and will, that for His sake they should be pardoned and saved.

So then by being reconciled to God by the death of his Son, we are saved by His life.

Use 1. By way of *Instruction* or *Information*.

Instruction 1. *Hence we must conclude, that Jesus Christ is most worthy of Honor*. It is a blessed and most honorable thing to be an instrument of making peace between brethren, between man and man who are at variance; how much more is it honorable to be the great instrument of settling an everlasting peace between God and man! The office of a mediator is in itself honorable. So does the Scripture speak of it as a great matter: "Is it a light thing that you should be My Servant, to raise up the tribes of Jacob, and to restore the preserved of Israel? I will also give you for a light to the Gentiles, that you may be my salvation to the ends of the earth" (Is. 49:6). To be an instrument of saving one soul, is a great honor: But what then is it to be the great cause of the salvation of millions of souls! even of all the elect, as Jesus Christ is, without whom never any of them had been saved.

Christ as mediator, has honorable titles given to Him in the Scriptures. Those names of *prophet*, *priest*, and *king*, are all of them honorable names. He is also, as mediator styled the "everlasting Father" (Is. 9:6). The Greek interpreters render those words, "the Father of the world to come." Christ as mediator is the Father of the *new world*: Adam is the father of the *old, ruined* world. But Christ the second Adam is the Father of the restored, redeemed world. His people especially have cause to honor him. They can never honor him enough who has ventured Himself; yes, and has cast His own body and soul into the flames of divine wrath, so that He might appease that Wrath and quench those flames on their behalf. Christ as Mediator is indeed inferior to the Father, but He is superior to every creature in earth or in heaven. Therefore, they all worship the Lamb that was slain, because *He is worthy.*

And the day is coming when "every knee shall bow" to the authority of Christ, and that considered as Jesus the mediator. It has been disputed among divines whether Christ as mediator be an object of divine worship; I see not how this argument for the affirmative can well be answered. The object of faith is an object of religious worship, for faith is internal worship. Nor may we believe or place the confidence of our souls in any other object besides what we may pray unto. But Christ as mediator is the proper and immediate object of faith. It is not enough for men to believe in God, except they believe in Christ, and so in God through the mediator (John 14:1).

Instruction 2. *Great is their sin who make into themselves other mediators besides Christ.* They rob Christ of his chief glory. Herein was the great and grossest superstition of the Gentiles of old, that they fancied and worshiped many mediators, demons or middle gods. They looked upon the souls of their heroes or deceased warriors to be demons, or agents between the sovereign deity and them. And this is the great idolatry of the apostate Christians, (i.e. the Papists); their idolatry does consist chiefly in their "doctrine of demons" (1 Tim. 4:1). Indeed, they do in words acknowledge that there is no mediator of redemption or satisfaction but Christ, and yet they think to satisfy for their own sins themselves, by their doing penance. And they pray for salvation on account of such a saint, or such a martyr. And they teach that there are more mediators of intercession than one. But that is contrary to clear Scripture. Hence the apostle having him speaking about intercession says, "there is one mediator" (1 Tim. 2:1, 5). None but Christ sits in the throne of God. Though believers shall sit in Christ's throne at the last day, yet none but Christ shall sit in God's throne (Rev. 3:21). Hence none else is to be the agent between God and all the elect.

It is an encroaching on Christ's royal prerogative, and therefore, derogatory to exalt any other to that dignity. It belongs to Christ as exalted to the right hand (or throne) of the Father, there to present our devotions to the "Father of glory" (Rom. 8:34). As none but the high priest might enter into the holy place; so it belongs to Christ alone to be a mediator in heaven. He appears for us as our agent. We have no other agent in heaven but Christ; none else to appear for us there (Heb. 9:24; Rev. 8:3). Therefore, for men to offer up prayers to any but Christ, and to God in Him, is heinous idolatry. It is true, that we may desire good men on earth to pray for us, but it does not therefore, follow that we may pray to them, as prayer is taken for religious worship. Nor does it follow, that because we may desire men on earth to pray for us, we may desire those in Heaven to do so; for they in heaven cannot hear us. If we desire them to do this or that, they know not what we say. As for the

Papists, there are thousands, it may be millions of them, praying at once to the virgin Mary. It is impossible that she being a creature only, should hear all those prayers at once. This is to turn Christ out of His office, and to place another in His room.

Use 2. *Let it be for conviction and awakening to all Christless ones.* They are without a mediator. There is none to stand between their souls and infinite justice, between them and everlasting burnings. Therefore, Christless sinners are in a miserable perishing estate. For Awakening here:

Consideration 1. *That no one can know that Christ has or will mediate for him, till he does truly believe.* Though it be true that Christ does mediate for his elect before their conversion (as was said), and hence it is that they are not cut off while in a state of unbelief; yet they cannot know nor be assured of this as long as they remain without Christ. For the elect of God are visibly in the same state with reprobates until Christ be formed in them (2 Cor. 13:5). Nor can they know their election before their "effectual vocation" (2 Pet. 1:10). A poor Christless creature, when he lies down at night, he knows not but that he may be in hell before morning when morning comes. He knows not but that he may be in hell before night; how sad is that! For a man to have the life of his body hang in doubt is very uncomfortable, but this man is a thousand times more miserable, the life of whose immortal soul is uncertain.

Consideration 2. *Every Christless sinner is under a sentence of death and wrath.* He is a poor condemned creature. "He that believeth not, is condemned already" (John 3:18). So that if death come upon him while in his Christless estate, he is as sure to be damned as if he were already in hell. Oh, Christless sinner, look about you and see where you are! Your soul is hanging over the mouth of hell by the rotten thread of a frail life. If that break, the devouring gulf will swallow you up for ever. The sentence is already passed upon you by that God who is the judge of all; and that which you are sentenced unto, is to lie and die under infinite wrath throughout the ages of eternity. "He that believes not, the wrath of God abides on him" (John 3:36). And can you bear that wrath? Who can stand before his indignation? They that have felt only a few scalding drops of that wrath falling upon their souls have thought it intolerable. "A wounded spirit who can bear?" (Prov. 18:14). If drops be so terrible, what will it be when a sea of wrath shall overwhelm the soul! If a few sparks of this wrath are so fearful, can your heart endure when you shall be thrown in the ocean of fire never to be quenched? Yet this is that which every Christless sinner is doomed unto.

Consideration 3. *There is no escaping this wrath without an interest in CHRIST.* None but JESUS can deliver from the wrath to come (1 Thes. 1:16). All the world cannot save you without Christ. They that were stung with the fiery deadly serpents in the wilderness, except they looked unto the brazen serpent died of their wounds. The deadly stings of sin are in your soul, if JESUS the mediator does not heal you, there is no remedy, but you must die. In vain will it be to hope for salvation in any other way men that are dying, are ready to catch at anything to save their lives; So it is with poor, perishing, damning souls; they are ready to lay hold on their duties, good meanings, anything to save them. "But in vain is salvation hoped for from the hills and the multitude of mountains" (Jer. 3:23). Nothing without Jesus the mediator ever did or can save a soul from death and wrath.

Consideration 4. *They that have heard of a mediator, and yet live and die in a Christless estate, will, of all creatures in the world, be most miserable forever.* They are most inexcusable. They have no cloak for their sin. Their souls are naked to the lashes of divine vengeance (John 15:22). There have been thousands of millions that have gone down into eternal darkness who never heard of JESUS the mediator. But their condemnation will not be so dreadful at the last day as of them that lived under the *gospel*; and had the offer of Christ and life set before them, but they chose death rather than life, sin rather than Christ. It will be more tolerable for the vilest wretch in Sodom at the Day of Judgment than for such Christ-despisers (Matt. 10:15). Oh, to despise a mediator is such a sin as there is none like unto it. If he that despised Moses' law died without mercy, of how much sorer punishment do you suppose he shall be thought worthy who has trodden underfoot the Son of God? If they escaped not who refused him that spoke on earth, much more shall we not escape if we turn away from Him that speaks from heaven.

Do not think now to ward off the blow, and to stave off convictions by saying, "we are all Christians, we all have an interest in Christ." Oh that it were so! Oh that there were not one Christless sinner in the congregation! But for the Lord's sake deceive not your own souls. "What communion has Christ with Belial?" (2 Cor. 6:15) "If men say they have Fellowship with him, and yet walk in darkness, the truth is not in them" (1 John 1:6). "They that are Christ's have crucified the flesh with the affections and lusts" (Gal. 5:24), "Yes, If any man be in Christ, he is a new creature" (2 Cor. 5:17). Let every soul then that is not, become a new creature, receive conviction, and be awakened with the sense of their misery. Awake you that sleep, and rise from the dead, and Christ shall give you light!

*Use 3. Here is matter of glorious consolation, and encouragement unto those that come to Jesus Christ.* There is admirable sweetness and consolation in these three words: JESUS THE MEDIATOR. The sum and sweetness of the gospel is contained in this, that *Jesus is the mediator.* I shall mention here some (and but a few of many) comfortable considerations which flow and follow from the doctrine of Christ's mediation.

*Consideration 1. It is hence evident that the work of redemption and salvation is put into a sure and able hand.* Into a hand that is able to go through with it. "He is mighty to save" (Zeph. 3:17); "He is able to save to the uttermost" (Heb. 7:25). You, a sinner, have destroyed yourself to the uttermost. You have stabbed your soul to death a thousand times over. How long has your soul lain dead in hell! Well but Christ can save you *over and over again*, notwithstanding all those deaths which your sins have brought upon you. Indeed, if the work of salvation were in any other hand it would miscarry. No mere man or angel could go through with it. But since it is in the hand of Jesus Christ the Son of God, there is no fear of miscarriage. If it were trusted in any other hand, woe would be to you and to me, and to all the world forever. But it is not possible it should miscarry in Christ's hand (Acts 2:24). Now this is a great comfort. Suppose a man to be miserably in debt; if a surety interpose that is able to pay the debt, that is a comfort to him. Even so is the case here.

Consideration 2. *Jesus Christ is a willing mediator.* Poor souls are apt to be discouraged, not so much in respect of the power of Christ which they do not doubt, as from His will to save them. They are ready to say as the leper did, "Lord, if you will you can make me clean" (Matt. 8:2). But know, Christ is willing to reconcile you to God if you are willing to be reconciled to Him. Christ by his messengers, beseeches sinners to be reconciled unto God. He began the work of mediation at first most willingly. He has gone through the greatest and heaviest part of His work with much willingness. He laid down His life of Himself, there was none took it from Him against his will. That work of suffering for sin and satisfying divine justice is done, and therefore, we may be sure, He is willing to attend what remains respecting the work of intercession. If you are a comer to Him, He is willing to intercede for you. He is ready to put in a good word for you in heaven before the Father of glory. He lives for that end (Heb. 7:25).

Consideration 3. *Now there is a mediator for poor sinners whose mediation is meritorious.* It is so because, Jesus is the mediator. There is merit in the blood of Christ, for He is the Son of God. Had we none but saints or angels to mediate for us, we were in a sad case, because they cannot merit. But Christ has merited all saving good for all His. He is a redeemer by price. As for the elect, He has bought every one of them, body and soul (1 Cor. 6:20). Yes, and he has bought heaven for them too, which is therefore, called the "purchased possession" (Eph. 1:14). And Christ is now interceding in heaven through the merit of His blood. Hence His blood is said to speak; so says the apostle here, "it speaks better things than the blood of Abel" (Heb. 12:24). It has a loud cry with it; a louder cry than

## MEDIATOR

that of Abel's blood; and yet that cried so as that it was heard from earth to heaven. Abel's blood cried for vengeance, Christ's blood cries for pardon. The blood of Christ cries louder than the law, or than sin the strength of the Law; which if it were not for sin would be able to hurt no man. The law cries and says, "This is a poor guilty sinner, let him be condemned forever." But if he be a believing sinner, the blood of Christ cries louder and says, "All his sins are satisfied for, and therefore let him be pardoned, and his soul live forever."

Consideration 4. *That both the person and the prayers of the comer to Christ shall find acceptance through Him who is the mediator.* His person is accepted in the beloved. Christ has brought him to be one of heaven's favorites. By Him we have access unto the Father. Jesus the Son of God does as it were take the believing soul by the hand, and leads him into the presence chamber. He opens the door for him and presents him before the Father of glory and says, "behold Oh Father, here is a soul that I died for. This soul is washed in my blood, and therefore, look upon him with a favorable eye for my sake." And the *prayers* of one that comes to Christ, and unto God by Him, will find acceptance in heaven. God says to such a soul as that great king said to Esther: "What is your petition, and it shall be granted to you; what is your request, and it shall be performed" (Es. 7:2). Indeed, if a man come to God without Christ, let him not think that he shall receive anything. Under the law, if a sacrifice was offered, and not first brought to the priest, it would not find acceptance; so if men offer up prayers or praises, and not by Christ, they will never be accepted by God. But come in Christ's name, and then ask as great things as you will or can (according to the will of God) and you need not doubt acceptance with him. The children of God are many times much discouraged because of the weakness of their prayers, but as long as we have such an one as Jesus to be our mediator, we may humbly hope for acceptance in heaven. Our prayers are poor vile things as proceeding from us, but the intercession of Christ is perfect and glorious. "Let us therefore, come boldly to the throne of grace, that we may obtain mercy, and find grace to help in a time of need" (Heb. 4:16).

Use 4. *Let us bless God for Christ; bless God for the mediator.* This is the most gladsome tidings that ever was heard of in the world. How did the angels rejoice and glorify God when Christ was born! One of them said to the shepherds, "'Behold I bring you good tidings of great joy, unto you this day is born a Savior which is Christ the Lord.' And suddenly there was with the angel a multitude of the heavenly host, praising God, and saying, 'glory be to God in the highest, and on earth peace; good will towards men'" (Luke 2:10-14). Shall they bless God because there is a Savior come into the world; and shall not men do so much more, as being more concerned in this good news than the angels are? This world is full of troubles: sad news comes from day to day. But here is good news from the heaven of heavens, that there is a JESUS, that there is a MEDIATOR. Had it not been for this mediator, every soul of us must have perished. There is no ascending into heaven but by Jacob's ladder, whose bottom was on earth, and the top of it in heaven (Gen. 24:14). This is true concerning the mediation of Christ. Had not the Son of God taken upon Him the office of a mediator, it would have puzzled men and angels to have answered Eli's question: "If a man sin against the Lord, who shall entreat for him?" (1 Sam. 2:25). When man had forsaken God, heaven and earth forsook him, and left him to shift for himself.

Now, that the Lord should look after lost man, when sin and guilt, and wrath and hell, and devils, and all the powers of darkness had fallen upon him, is wonderful to consider. Oh, bless His name; the mediator has stepped in between our souls and everlasting burnings. So that now we who have been great sinners may draw nigh to God with a humble boldness, and commune with Him who is upon the mercy seat. If you are a true believer, you may think of the Day of Judgment with unspeakable joy (1 John 4:17). Why? He that shall be your judge is your Savior, your Redeemer, your Mediator. Though we have to do with God the judge of all, we need not fear, since we are come to JESUS the mediator of the new covenant. What, shall I say more? By means of Christ the mediator, believers are made happier than Adam was. One of the ancients said truly, that "Job on the dunghill was happier than Adam in paradise." Adam lost his happiness, but this the believer can never do. That heaven which Christ has prepared for believers is a far better place than the earthly paradise was. Adam in his first estate was made lower than the angels: he stood in need of meat and drink and sleep, and so should all his children have done, in case he (and they all in him) had never sinned. But as for believers, before Christ has done with them, He will make them equal with angels. At the resurrection their bodies shall be spiritualized, and immortalized, that they cannot die anymore. And their souls shall be filled with divine knowledge and grace, beyond what the soul of Adam was in his first estate. And their glory shall never fade away. And all this because of Jesus the mediator of the New Covenant. Oh then, bless God for Jesus Christ; which to do will be the work of heaven throughout the days of eternity.

# 7
# God the Father Is Fully Satisfied by the Obedience of Jesus Christ

> "This is my beloved Son,
> in whom I am well pleased."
> Matthew 3:17

In this chapter, there are two things contained. First, a sermon preached by John Baptist whereby he does prepare his auditors[50] for Christ. Second, the history of Christ's baptism: and under that the evangelist has recorded three miraculous providences, which did at that time come to pass:

1. *The opening of the heavens* (Matt. 3:15). No doubt but the heavens were really opened by the infinite power of the almighty; whereby may be signified, that heaven which was shut against all the children of fallen man, is opened to them now *in* and *by* Jesus Christ.

2. *Another miraculous thing which did attend the baptism of Christ was, that the Holy Ghost did visibly descend upon Him like a dove.* And this might be, so that the prophesy of Isaiah might be fulfilled literally as well as spiritually: "The Spirit of the Lord is come upon me" (Is. 61:1), and also, thereby to intimate how Christ was filled was the spirit of innocence and meekness.

---

[50] Listeners.

3. *There was a miraculous voice which came from God out of heaven*; and that is expressed in this verse, wherein we have a most glorious, divine testimony concerning Christ. God from heaven does here testify two things of Him:

(1) That He is *His Son*, yes, His *beloved* Son. He is so His Son, as none else is; so beloved, as none else is. Angels are the sons of God, but they only in respect of creation. Believers are the sons of God, but in respect of adoption, whereas Christ is not the son of God on those accounts, but in respect of nature. And therefore, Jesus Christ is dearer to God than all saints and angels.

(2) God does here testify concerning his Son Jesus Christ, that He is *well pleased in Him*. Now this pleasure of the Father in Christ, does intimate not only, that God takes infinite delight in Christ, (though that be part of what is intended; these words alluding to Isaiah 42:1 and 62:4, but also that the Father has received satisfaction in and by Jesus Christ. Hence, it is not said I am well pleased *with Him*, but *in Him*. That is to say God is pacified in and by Jesus Christ. When He beholds Christ, He lays aside all his indignation, and looks upon His people with a most favorable aspect. These words do show, that the revenging wrath of God is forever appeased, and His justice fully satisfied by the interposition and mediation of Jesus Christ.

*God the Father has received full satisfaction*
*in the obedience of His Son Jesus Christ.*[51]

---

[51] Samuel Rutherford, *The Covenant of Life Opened* (Edinburgh: Printed by Andro Anderson for Robert Brown, 1655), 206–209, 225–230; Herman Bavinck, *Reformed Dogmatics, Vol. 3: Sin and Salvation*

In order to the clearing of this doctrine, three things may be attended. First, to show that there is a *necessity* of this thing, that God should be satisfied for the wrong done to Him by the sins of His people. Second, that Jesus Christ has *satisfied* the Father. Third, the reasons of this doctrine; whence it is, that the obedience of Jesus Christ is satisfactory.

### There was a necessity of this satisfaction[52]

We shall mention two heads of arguments which do evince the truth of this.

First, it is evident in that *God has decreed and declared that sin shall be punished.* There is an eternal decree concerning this thing. Now upon a supposition of the decree of God that sin shall be punished, it necessarily follows that the event will be accordingly. For the decrees of God are unchangeable; hence are they fitly compared "to mountains of brass" (Zech. 6:1). Also, this decree is published, namely, in the written law (Gal. 3:10). Yes, when God made man at first, He did peremptorily[53] declare that sin should be punished with death (Gen. 2:17). Wherefore the apostle says that, "it is appointed unto men once to die" (Heb. 9:27). There is a statute law which must take place as seen earlier in Genesis 2:17. So it cannot stand

---

*in Christ* (Grand Rapids: Baker Academic, 2006), 340-353,377-406; John Calvin, *Institutes of the Christian Religion* (Peabody: Hendrickson, 2008), 323-343.

[52] Hugo Grotius, *Truth of the Christian Religion in Six Books* (Grand Rapids: Christian Classics Ethereal Library, 1829), Book 2; Anthony Burgess, *The True Doctrine of Justification Asserted and Vindicated* (London: First Ed. 1648); John Owen: *Exposition in Hebrews 2:10* (Edinburgh: Banner of Truth, 1992), Volume 3.

[53] Decisively, absolutely.

with the wisdom nor with the veracity of God to pardon sin without satisfaction; He having decreed and declared otherwise.

A second demonstration is, that *God's punishing sin does proceed not only from His will, but from His nature*. Hence there was a necessity of satisfaction. If God punish sin only voluntarily, there would not be such a necessity of satisfaction as indeed there is. Wherefore it is from the nature and essential justice of God that sin is punished, as appears:

(1) *In that when the Scripture speaks of God's punishing sin, it is ascribed not only to his will, but to his just nature* (Ps. 11:6-7). The Psalmist gives it as the reason why God does punish the wicked, even because He is righteous. The nature of God is such, as that He cannot but love righteousness, and so hate and punish wickedness (Rev. 16:5; 2 Thes. 1:6).

(2) It is evident in that God is the supreme governor and judge of all (Gen. 18:25; Rom. 3:5-6). God has not only an absolute sovereignty over His creatures in respect whereof He may punish or spare, kill, or keep alive; but He is moreover a judge, in respect whereof it is necessary He should punish the guilty. It is necessary to a judge to punish where the law requires him so to do. Now, what law is to another judge who is to proceed by it, that is the infinite rectitude of God's own nature to Him. Though the Lord's dominion be absolute, yet He does not rule arbitrarily, without respect to any rule or law. But that God should have any external law prescribed to Him in the government of the world is infinitely impossible. Therefore, His law is the righteousness of His own nature. Hence it is nec-

essary, that in dealing with His creatures, He should act according to that, and therefore, manifest indignation against sin. God in punishing sin, is considered not only as an offended person, but as an offended judge, which cannot but do that which is right, and ought to be done.

(3) *The infinite holiness of the blessed God does punish sin not only from His will but His nature* (1 Sam. 2:2; Rev. 15:4). Hence God is said to "hate sin" (Ps. 5:4). Yes, and this displicency[54] against sin is natural unto the blessed God. He cannot but hate sin. It is inconsistent with the holy nature of God, to love any sin, or not to hate every sin. It is not said that God will not, but that "He cannot look upon iniquity" (Hab. 1:13). He cannot approve of it; which evinces that sin is contrary to the nature of God, and that the purity of His nature does require that sin should be duly punished. And it is on the account of the infinite holiness of God that He is compared to a "consuming fire" (Is. 33:15), because it is natural to God (acting nevertheless as a free and intellectual agent) to hate and punish sin.

(4) *The common suffrage of mankind does give in evidence to this truth, that such is the nature of God, that sin must of necessity be satisfied for.* There is such an innate principle as this engraved upon the very conscience of men, that God will punish sin. Hence the apostle speaking concerning the generality of the Gentiles says as in Romans 1:32, "Who knowing the judgment of God, that they which commit such things are worthy of death." They knew that God judged this necessary to be done, even that sin should be punished with death. Hence even

---

[54] Aversion, dissatisfaction.

those barbarians could say, (as in Acts 28:4) "vengeance will not suffer him to live." They looked upon vengeance [*ekdikesis*] as a deity that would surely find out sinners that deserved death, but escaped it from the hands of men. Such a notion was implanted in their minds, that, there is a God who will take vengeance for sin. From this it came to pass that the Gentiles had so many sacrifices, thinking that this would pacify a provoked God. And from this principle it is, that the consciences of sinners do secretly sting them and condemn them when they do evil in the sight of God (Rom. 2:15). Now conscience is a man's judging of himself, as God will judge him forever. Yes, and from this principle it is, that when men do apprehend themselves any ways injured, they appeal to God to right them. Surely, there would not be such a presumption in the minds of all men that God will punish sin, if His punishing thereof did proceed merely from an act of His will, and not from an essential property of His nature. For the acts of God's will which are merely such are not known but by revelation; whereas this, that God will punish sin, is known by the light of nature without any special revelation, which shows that it proceeds not merely from the will, but from the righteous nature of God.

(5) *If God's punishing sin be merely from His will, then it would follow, that He is as free to reward sin as to punish it.* That sin or no sin is all one to him: for all the merely free acts of God's will might have been otherwise. And then, whereas He does will men to love and serve Him, He might have willed them to hate and oppose Him, and that no punishment should have been due to them on the account of any disobedience. But this cannot stand with the nature of God.

(6) *God would not have caused Christ to have suffered such bitter things if there had not been a necessity of satisfaction.* Would God have caused His only begotten Son to come into the world and to die such an accursed death to save sinners, if there had been a possibility of pardon and salvation without satisfaction (Rom. 8:32)? These things then make it appear that God does naturally and necessarily punish sin. Only we must know that when God is said naturally to punish sin, natural is not to be taken in every respect in that sense as when it is said, that it is natural for the fire to burn, or the like: as if God should necessarily punish sin as soon as it is committed or to the utmost of His power. But natural is taken in that sense as when we say it is natural to a man to speak, or laugh, or weep; but the exercise of these properties which are natural is subject to wisdom and liberty. Also, one may be said to act freely, that yet upon supposition of this or that does act necessarily. God always acts freely in whatever He does. It is free to Him to speak to his creatures or not to speak to them, but upon supposition that He will do so, it is necessary that He should speak truth, nor can he speak otherwise (2 Tim. 2:13; Tit. 1:2; Heb. 6:18).

We come now to the second thing propounded in order to the doctrine before us, that is to show:

## Christ has satisfied the Father for the wrong that has been done by the sins of His people

This is a great mystery of the gospel and all the knowledge we have about it is supernatural. The light of nature discovers nothing about this. The light of nature discovers that satisfaction is necessary, yet not how or which way this should be effected. Thence the Gentiles knew the former, but were ignorant of this latter, albeit some of them thought it must be *cruore humano*— by the death of a man. Only the Scriptures do most clearly and abundantly reveal this truth. We shall therefore keep close to the Scripture in producing arguments for the confirmation of the doctrine before us.

Argument 1. *All those Scriptures which speak of God being pacified by Christ, prove that he has satisfied the Father.* For that is intended by the satisfaction of Christ, namely, that He has done that whereby God is pacified towards His people; all their sins and injuries offered to Him thereby, notwithstanding. But this the Scripture speaks abundantly of. Hence God is said to be pleased in and by Him, as we have heard the text before us expressing. Hence, we read of "reconciliation" by Christ (2 Cor. 5:19; Rom. 5:10), and of "peace with God" through Christ (Rom. 5:1; Col. 1:20), and of "atonement" by Christ (Rom. 5:11), and of Christ's being a "propitiation" (Rom. 3:25; 1 John 2:2). Because in and by Jesus Christ, God does become propitious (i.e. favorable towards sinners). God had a controversy with all the world for sin; but as for the elect of God, Christ has come and taken up that controversy, appeased the wrath, and obtained the favour of God. Therefore, we are said to be reconciled and at peace with God by Jesus Christ.

Argument 2. *All those Scriptures which speak of Jesus Christ's being offered on the account of the sins of His people, evince the truth of this doctrine of Christ's SATISFACTION.* For that was the end of Christ's being made an offering for sin, that satisfaction to divine justice might thereby be accomplished. In the Scriptures Christ is said to be an "oblation" (Heb. 9:28; 10:10), and "sacrifice" (Heb. 9:26; 1 Cor. 5:7). On the same account Christ is called a "lamb" (John 1:29), and an "altar"

(Heb. 13:10). And this was the great intendment of all sacrifices under the law, even to hold forth the satisfaction of Christ. When they were offered, God was pacified towards His sinning people: "If the Lord have stirred you up against me, let Him accept an offering" (1 Sam. 26:19; see also 2 Sam. 24:25) (i.e. Let Him be appeased or satisfied therewith). "The Lord smelled a sweet savor" (Gen. 8:21). This expression intimates that God was well pleased with that offering. Now those sacrifices could not of themselves satisfy or appease the wrath of God, and it was not possible that they should (Heb. 10:4) as they were only types of Christ, and did put the Lord in mind of the sacrifices of the New Testament in due time to be offered. God was pacified towards believers under the Old Testament on the account of this sacrifice which was to take place when the fullness of time should come (Heb. 9:15).

Argument 3. *All those Scriptures which speak of Christ's being a redeemer, do evince the doctrine of His satisfaction to divine justice* (Tit. 2:14). For Christ is a redeemer, not only by *power* but by *price*. Hence His people are said to be bought by him, yes, "bought with a price" (1 Cor. 6:20; 7:23). Nothing can be spoken more clearly and expressly to prove that Christ is a redeemer, not by power only, but by price also. Hence the elect of God are said to be "ransomed" (Matt. 20:28; 1 Tim. 2:6). The Greek word [*antilutron*] there used, signifies the laying down of a just valuable price, even as much as the thing is worth. Jesus Christ, the Son of God, has given as much as all the lives and the souls of His people are worth, so that He might redeem them from that misery which they were justly condemned unto.

Argument 4. *All those Scriptures which speak of sins being done away by the blood of Christ, prove that His death was satisfactory.* Hence the sins of His people are said to be "purged" away thereby (Heb. 1:3), and "washed away" (Rev. 1:5), and their souls "sprinkled" therewith to the cleansing of them from the guilt and filth of sin (Heb. 10:22). That which does avail to the removing of the guilt of sin, and so of the punishment due thereunto, is satisfactory to divine justice, but this we see is true of the death of Christ.

Argument 5. *All those Scriptures which speak of Christ's standing in our stead prove the doctrine of His satisfaction to divine justice.* He stands *in our stead.* He is called a "surety" (Heb. 7:22) and is said to "die" for us (2 Cor. 5:14-15), (i.e. not only for our benefit but in our room; for us instead of us), (2 Sam. 18:33; Rom. 5:6-7). Hence Christ is said to die not only for us, but for our sins (1 Cor. 15:3). A substitution of one in the room of another is noted by that expression. The apostles and martyrs all died for our good, but not for our sins; as it is said of Christ. Therefore, that expression of Christ's dying for us, implies more than His dying for our benefit only. And He is said to be a "curse" for us (Gal. 3:13), the curse which was due to us fell upon Him, and He "bore our sins" (1 Pet. 2:24; Is. 53:11). The Hebrew word [Sabal] signifies such a bearing as implies burden, or punishment, and is never used in any other sense. If we consult the Scriptures we shall find that the meaning of bearing sins, is to undergo the punishment due for sin (Lam. 5:7; Num. 14:33; Ezek. 18:26). Hence it is that we escape destruction, and this is all that is intended by the doctrine of Christ's satisfaction, namely, that He has undergone the punishment which was due to us, whence God is satisfied so as to let us escape with our lives. Thus is the word satisfaction used in the Scripture (Num. 35:31-32). And it is a full satisfaction which Christ has made. He has cleared all accounts between God and His elect. Therefore, He said "the Spirit shall convince the world of righteousness: because I go to my Father and you see me no more" (John 16:10). We may be sure that Christ has done the work which God sent him into the world for to the full satisfaction of the Father; that He has made reconciliation for sin, and brought in everlasting righteousness. Otherwise when He came to heaven, His Father would not have entertained Him at His own right hand but have sent Him into the world again.

We come in the third place to enquire into the *reasons of this doctrine*. We shall mention but two. The first shall be taken from the dignity of Christ's Person; the second from the perfection of His obedience.

Reason 1. *From the dignity of Christ's person.* He is the Son of God, as the text, expresses; and thence a person of infinite worth and dignity, which does add value to His sufferings and satisfaction. It is true that the human nature only suffered (if we speak strictly), all passion being incompatible to the divine nature, nevertheless by reason of the personal union between the two natures of Christ, that which does properly belong to one nature is truly affirmed of the person. It is therefore most true that the second person of the Trinity, even the Son of God Himself, became subject to the penalty of the law in order to appease of the wrath and satisfy the justice of the Father, who was the person directly offended by sin. What Christ has done in order to salvation, He did as mediator; and therefore, not as

God only nor as man only but as Godman. Now for such a person to become subject to the penalty of the law, and to the wrath of God, is (as I have elsewhere expressed), more than if all men and angels had lain under His wrath throughout the days of eternity. Therefore, well might the Lord say that He was pleased in or pacified by His Son Jesus Christ.

Reason 2. *From the perfection of Christ's obedience. His active obedience was perfect, He did fulfill all that the Law required to be done* (Matt. 3:15). He never did transgress the law in any one particular. Though He lived in this world for the space of thirty years and upwards, yet He never did commit the least sin, in thought, word, or deed. Such a high priest became us, who is holy, harmless, and separate from sinners. And as to that singular law of a redeemer, He did yield perfect obedience thereunto. Hence was His passive obedience. It was not the moral law but that special law of a redeemer which required that Christ should become subject unto death. And thus was He obedient to the very utmost extent of this law (Phil. 2:7).

Some have objected: "But, we are saved by grace, how then is satisfaction made for the wrong that we have done? Is the debt paid and then forgiven? This is strange kind of grace," say the Socinians.

Answer: *Grace may well stand with the satisfaction of Christ.* The apostle thought so when he said that, we are justified freely by grace, and yet that it is in a way of redemption, (or that a price is paid for it) through Jesus Christ (Rom. 3:23-25). Not only justice but grace is set in the throne in this way of salvation by the obedience and satisfaction of Christ (See Rom. 5). For it was grace to accept of the satisfaction of another. In that respect there was some relaxation of the rigour of the law. It was from the grace and loving kindness of God, that He found out this way of salvation; men and angels could never have found such a way if the Lord Himself had not done it. It was infinite grace that sent Christ into the world; so that He might satisfy and merit on the behalf of those for whom He died. We must not under pretense of exalting free grace, rob God of the glory of His justice and righteousness. When men say that God is merciful, and therefore, they may be saved though they should not repent and believe, they do under pretense of magnifying mercy, rob God of the glory of His truth and holiness. So it is when men deny the satisfaction of Christ, under pretense of being saved by mercy.

Use. Let it be a word of exhortation. *Let us make sure of an interest in the glorious satisfaction which Christ has made.* Therefore:

Consideration 1. *That an interest herein is absolutely necessary.* For God is displeased and His wrath incensed by the sins of men. That wrath which burns to the bottom of hell is kindled against your soul, and nothing but the blood of Christ can quench that infinite flame. God has said "the soul that sins shall die" (Ezek. 18:20). There never was one sin committed since the world began (nor ever shall be) which shall escape unpunished. Sin will be punished either in Him who is the surety for believing sinners, or in the sinner himself to eternity. Satisfaction is necessary, nor is there any other way of satisfaction to the justice of God, but only this. All a man's own righteousness will avail nothing as to satisfaction for transgressions that are past. Prayers and duties can do nothing as to this matter.

Though the prayers and services of believers please God, yet they do not appease Him (Mic. 6:6), nor tears either (Jer. 2:22). Though a poor creature should wash himself in tears, could he bathe his soul in tears, all would not avail to purge away so much as one sin. "The sin of Judah is written with a pen of iron, and graven with the point of a diamond" (Jer. 17:1). Letters which are written in glass with the point of a diamond, all the washing in the world cannot get them out again; so are the sins of men engraved upon their souls in black and bloody characters. Nothing but the blood of Christ can wash away the stain and guilt thereof. All men and angels can never satisfy for one sin.

Hence it comes to pass that the misery of the damned is ETERNAL, because they are never able to make full satisfaction to the glorious justice of the holy God, who has been wronged and offended by the sins of men.

Consideration 2. *The blessed condition they are in who have a real interest in this satisfaction.* God is pleased with them; for He is more pleased with the righteousness of Christ, than ever He was displeased with the disobedience of men. Christ has pleased God more than all the sins of the elect have provoked him (Rom. 5:19; John 10:10). It is a full and perfect satisfaction which Christ has made, so as that He has left nothing for anyone to come and do after Him (Heb. 7:25). The bill is canceled even the handwriting which was against us (Col. 2:14).

Rule. 1. *Look for salvation nowhere else but in Christ* (Is. 55:3). Do not think by future duties to make amends to God for former iniquities. The Papists teach men to look for satisfaction through their *own* works; in penances, prayers, fastings, self-macerations,[55] supererogations[56] etc. But as the apostle said to the Galatians, "If you be circumcised, Christ will profit you nothing" (Gal. 5:2); so I say, if you think to satisfy the justice, or appease the wrath of God, by any righteousness of your own, the satisfaction of Christ will profit you nothing.

*Rule. 2. Believe on Jesus Christ the Son of God, and then you shall have an interest in His righteousness and satisfaction* (Rom. 3:25). From the moment that the soul does truly close with Christ by faith unfeigned in His name, Christ and all His redeeming benefits becomes his forever. He has then an interest in the obedience, merit, and satisfaction of the LORD JESUS. And that God who said from heaven concerning Jesus Christ, "He is my beloved Son in whom I am well pleased" (Matt. 3:17), says to every such soul, "I am well pleased with you, in and through JESUS CHRIST."

---

[55] Self-denials.
[56] The performance of more work than duty requires.

# 8
# THE HUMAN NATURE OF CHRIST IS, OF ALL CREATED OBJECTS, THE MOST EXCELLENT & GLORIOUS

"You are fairer than the children of men."
Psalm 45:2

Concerning the penmen of this Psalm there is nothing certain to be determined. Some conjecture that Solomon wrote it as an epitome of his Song of Songs; this being altogether of the same nature with that. It is in the title said to be a *Song of Loves* (i.e. a *love song*). The Hebrews of old had their *epithalamia*[57]. It was a custom with them, that when persons of note were married, some composed songs in praise of the bride groom and the bride. The title of this Psalm alludes to that custom, so that what is here written is a spiritual love song, setting forth the praises of Christ and of his Church.

After the title we have: 1. The *Preface*, and 2. The *Matter of the Psalm*.

1. The *Preface* in verse 1 wherein are three particulars:
(1.) The quality of the matter here contained. It is called a good matter. The Hebrew phrase [*dabar Tob*] signifies a good

---

[57] A song or poem celebrating marriage.

word; intimating that the things contained therein are of singular worth and excellency.

(2.) The subject of this good matter: "touching the king"— which interpreters generally expound of King Solomon, but of him, only as a *type*. The Hebrew doctors themselves acknowledge that the King Messiah is here principally intended. And there are diverse passages in the Psalm which cannot be applied to Solomon, nor to any other person besides *Christ* and therefore, the apostle in the first chapter to the Hebrews quoting some expressions in this Psalm says they are meant of Christ the Son of God.

(3) He declares what were the instruments communicating this good matter concerning the King Christ; namely, His heart, and His tongue. "My heart is inditing"[58] (Ps. 45:2). The original word [*Racash*] signifies to *boil up*; alluding (as it seems) to the [*Mincah*] or meat offering under the law, which was boiled or fried with oil, and so offered to the Lord. Thus the Holy Spirit did as it were set the heart of the Psalmist on fire, and made it to boil up with holy and heart ravishing meditations concerning the glory of Christ. And then his tongue became as the pen of a ready writer (i.e. like one that writes *short hand*); and so will take every word that the inditer shall speak. His tongue would express all that the Holy Spirit should indite in his heart. Thus for the preface.

2. As for the *matter of the Psalm*, it does contain, a description of Christ in His glory and of the Church in her beauty.

In the words before us (which begin the matter of the Psalm) Christ is declared a superlatively excellent person, to be

---

[58] Writing, composing.

one of incomparable beauty and glory: "You are fairer." The Hebrew word [*Jophjaphitha*] is of a double form to note a perfect beauty, or beauty in the highest degree. And whereas the beauty of Christ is compared with and preferred to that of any of the children of men, that shows that the words are not to be interpreted of Christ in respect of his deity, for so His excellency admits of no comparison, but of Him as the son of man. It is meant of a communicated beauty, even a glory which the human nature of Christ is forever blessed with, as the last words in the verse intimate.

The doctrine at present to be insisted on is: *That the human nature of Jesus Christ, is of all created objects the most excellent and glorious.*

Here, two things may be enquired into: First, how it does appear, that the human nature of Christ, is, of all created objects the most excellent and glorious. Second, the reason why it is so.

## The Scriptures abundantly bear witness to the truth of this doctrine

Hence Christ is said to be anointed above all others. In the seventh verse of this Psalm it is said: "God your God has anointed you with the oil of gladness above your fellows." The human nature of Christ is a creature, but it has an anointing which makes it excel all its fellow creatures. Hence the man Christ Jesus is said to be: "The prince of the kings of the earth" (Rev. 1:5), (i.e. more excellent than any of them; never any of them was to compart with Him). Therefore, also, He is styled the "KING of Kings, and LORD of Lords"; that is to say, of all Kings, and of all Lords, the most excellent and glorious one (Rev. 19:16). And the Scripture says of the man Christ Jesus that, "He must in all things have the preeminence" (Col. 1:18). And that God has made Him His *firstborn* (Ps. 89:27), yes, that He is "the firstborn of every creature" (Col. 1:15). The firstborn had a privilege belonging to him above the rest of the children; so has the man Christ above all creatures; yes, above all men and angels. As the elect of God are styled "the Church of the firstborn" (Heb. 12:23), importing their dignity above others, so the man Christ Jesus is indeed the *firstborn* of the firstborn; the most excellent one of all those that are near and dear to God.

## Christ as man has a larger measure of the Holy Spirit than ever was communicated to any creature

In that respect He is said to be "anointed with oil above His fellows"; as in the Scripture but now mentioned. The oil which the Lord Christ was anointed with was none other but the oil of the Holy Spirit. "God anointed Jesus of Nazareth with the Holy Ghost and with power" (Acts 10:38). And another Scripture says "God gives the Spirit without measure unto Him" (John 3:34). Christ, considered as God, has not received anything, but as man, the Spirit is given to Him, and that without measure. Not that infinite perfections are communicated to the human nature (for that is not compatible to a creature nor is it possible that finite should be infinite), but there are no limits set thereunto. None can say in how great a measure Christ has received the Spirit. He has received thereof in such a measure as no man ever did; as large a measure of the Spirit as is possible to be communicated to a man or creature. Hence it is said that, "all fullness dwells in him." "For it pleased the Father that in Him all Fullness should dwell" (Col. 1:19). As for that fullness which dwells in Him as God, it cannot be said properly that it was the "pleasure of the Father" that it should be in Him.

But this is true with respect to the fullness which dwells in him as man and mediator. There is a fullness of spiritual gifts in the man Christ Jesus. He has a greater measure of wisdom and knowledge than every man or angel did attain unto. "In whom are hid all the treasures of wisdom and knowledge" (Col. 2:3). Treasures of wisdom, yes, all treasures thereof are in him (i.e. not only objectively in that the wisdom of God does appear in the mystery of Christ more than in any thing), but all treasures of wisdom are in Him subjectively. As man He has the vastest measure of knowledge that ever was contained in a finite understanding. It is written concerning Solomon, that he was wiser than all men, and that God gave him "understanding exceeding much, and largeness of heart even as the sand that is on the sea shore" (1 Kings 4:29), intimating that his enlarged understanding did comprehend a multitude of notions and conceptions in number like the sand of the sea. In that, Solomon was a type of Christ. Yet let me say, Solomon had a very shallow understanding and comprehension of things if compared with the man Christ Jesus. Christ's wisdom is a thousand times greater than ever Solomon's was, or than ever any other man attained unto.

And the soul of Christ is endowed and adorned with all spiritual graces, in the highest degree that can be. The prophet Isaiah saw the Lord sitting upon a throne, and His train filled the Temple. There are a train of glorious graces which fill the temple of Christ's human nature. There is no other man on earth or in heaven has so much grace but it is possible for him to have yet more; but the man Christ Jesus is so full of grace, as that it is impossible for Him to have more. "The Word was made flesh, and dwelt amongst us full of grace and truth. Yes, and of His fullness have all we received, and grace for grace" (John 1:14, 16). What a glorious and inexpressible fullness of grace is that! To have so much fullness of grace, as to be able to impart thereof to all the elect of God. Christ is as full of grace, as a fountain is full of water. Yes, as full of grace, as the sun is full of light; for which cause He is styled the "sun of righteousness" (Mal. 4:2). And He said of Himself, "I am the light of the world" (John 8:12).

There are some believers who have received a large measure of spiritual gifts and graces, but have it all from Christ. How full is He then! We read in Zechariah 4:11-12 of, "two olive trees by the candlestick, which empty the golden oil out of themselves." In the type, Joshua and Zerubbabel were the "sons of oil", who did improve the gifts and graces which they had received for the benefit of the candlestick of the Jewish Church. So Christ is always imparting of that fullness which He has received to believers, and to His Churches, through the golden pipes of His ordinances. Then what an unmeasurable fullness of the grace of the Spirit has the Lord Jesus received! There is in Christ an inexhaustible ocean of grace. Believers are said to have rivers of grace flowing into their hearts (John 7:38). But Christ has an ocean of grace flowing in His blessed heart. As all rivers come from the sea; so all those rivers of grace in the souls of believers are derived from that sea of grace which is in Jesus Christ.

**The man Christ Jesus is more like to God than may be affirmed of any other man or angel**
And indeed it must needs be so, because He has a greater intimacy of communion with God than ever man or creature had.

We read concerning Moses, that God spoke with him face to face as a man speaks with his friend; and the Lord said of him, "With him will I speak mouth to mouth, and the similitude of the Lord shall he behold" (Num. 12:8). Moses was in that thing a type of Christ, who has such familiarity with God the Father of glory as never any one else had. He is (to speak after the manner of men) God's privy counsellor. Wherefore it is said, "no man has seen God at any time (no not Moses himself so as Christ has seen Him) "the only begotten Son who is in the bosom of the Father, He has declared Him" (John 1:18).

Now Moses by conversing with God became more like Him than any other man; impressions of the divine glory were left upon his countenance. How much more is it true concerning the man Christ Jesus, who lies in the bosom of God the Father! "This man was counted worthy of more glory than Moses" (Heb. 3:3). Hence the apostle speaks of the "glory of God in the face of Jesus Christ" (2 Cor. 4:6). Says he, "the glory of God did appear in the face of Moses, but how much more in the face of Jesus Christ!" Yes, the man Christ Jesus is so like unto God, as that He is said to be His very image, "who is the image of the invisible God" (Col. 1:15). There is a double image of God; His essential image: so Christ as second person or Son of God is the image of the Father; and a manifestative image, so Christ as man is the image of God. "The end of an image is to make a thing apparent which otherwise would not be seen.

Now the Godhead which is invisible is made manifest in the human nature of Christ. Hence, He is said to be the image of the invisible God, intimating that the divine perfections are made visible in Christ so as is nowhere else to be seen.[59] Of all

---

[59] Thomas Goodwin, *Of the Knowledge of Christ*. (Edinburgh: Banner of Truth, 2015), Section 3, Chapter 2.

those perfections which are in the Godhead, Christ is the complete image above what angels and men are; and He makes those perfections visible to us, so as no mere creature does the like. Though the human nature of Christ does (and shall forever) remain in its properties really distinct from the divine nature, yet it does in divine properties and perfections resemble the Godhead more fully than any creature does or ever shall do. For example, omniscience is a divine property. Now, though the human nature of Christ is not (as Lutherans suppose) omniscient with the omniscience of the divine nature, yet there is a similitudinary omnisciency belonging thereto.

That which I intend is this: the human nature of Christ now glorified, knows all things that ever God has done since the world began; yes, and all that God will do; which is more than can be said of any other man or creature. There is not one believer in the world, nor one elect vessel in the world, but Christ as man and not as God only has the knowledge of Him. Wherefore the Scripture says that the Father "reveals all things to the Son; and shows Him whatever He does" (John 5:18). Christ as God has nothing revealed to Him, but as man all things are now showed unto Him. Again, omnipotence is a divine property; and there is a similitudinary omnipotence to be affirmed of the man Christ Jesus. Hence, He is said to be the "power of God" (1 Cor. 1:24), and "the arm of the Lord" (Is. 53:1). All that God means to do in the world, the man Christ Jesus is the instrument of effecting it. We may say the like with respect unto other divine attributes, they shine forth in the human nature of Christ more than anywhere; yes, more than in all the creatures in the whole world besides.

## Christ as man is made Lord of all (Heb. 1:2)

Christ as God has not an Heirship or Lordship appointed to him. He is heir of all things without any designation from the Father, but as man and mediator He is the appointed heir. God the Father has put the government of the whole world into the hands of that one man. "The Father judges no man; but has committed all judgment (i.e. all power of government) unto the Son" (John 5:22). It is true, that this power does not belong to Christ as man only, yet as man and not as God only. Therefore, in verse 27 it is said, "He has given him authority to execute judgment because He is the son of MAN." The Lord Christ has, (it is true) a peculiar dominion over His Church, which is therefore, by way of eminency called His Kingdom.

But He has moreover a providential kingdom, which does appertain unto Him as Godman. Hence Ezekiel in his vision of the wheel (by which we are to understand the wheel of providence) saw a "throne and the likeness as the appearance of a man above upon it" (Ezek. 1:26). The man Christ Jesus is co-partner with God in the government of the world. This mystery was signified by Solomon's sitting upon David's throne while his father was yet living (1 Kings 1:48). Therein he was a type of Christ who sits upon the throne of God His Father, as Himself declares, (saying) "I am set down with my Father in His throne" (Rev. 3:21). That this dominion does belong to Christ as man, is evident inasmuch as the Scripture says it is given to Him (Matt. 28:18). Christ as God has no power given to Him, but as man, all power in heaven and earth is given to Him (Matt. 11:27, John 3:35). This dominion was His due, as soon as ever He came into the world. He was born a King (Matt. 2:2).

But the man Christ Jesus did upon his entering into heaven actually undertake the government of the world. He does (to speak after the manner of men) ease the Father of that burden, and undertake to manage the government of the world for Him. This is a thing which no man nor angel but only the man Christ Jesus could undertake, nor was it possible for any other man to bear such a glory. Hence in Revelation 5:2 there is a proclamation to see who would take the book out of the hand of him that sits upon the throne. That book is a commission to fulfill and execute all the decrees of God which respect the government of the world until the Day of Judgment. None but the Lamb was found worthy or meet for this. But "He took the book" (i.e. He has undertaken the government of the world until all that God has decreed shall be accomplished). And in verse 5 "He opens the Book" (i.e. He sees to the fulfillment of all according to the mind of the Father). Hence all creatures are made subject to this man. The angels of heaven are the most glorious of all created beings, yet they are made subject to this man. "Jesus Christ is gone into heaven; angels, authorities and powers, being made subject unto Him" (1 Pet. 3:22). The highest angel in heaven, is no better than a servant to the man Christ Jesus. They go upon His errand wheresoever He is pleased to send them. And He declares from heaven to all the world, that the holy angels are His subjects and servants: "I, Jesus have sent mine angel" (Rev. 22:16). And this is a mystery which only the Scripture reveals unto us. The light of nature discovers unto us that God governs the world, but that God-man does so, is not known but by the gospel.

## Christ as man is the head of the elect

"Behold I lay in Zion a chief corner stone, elect, precious, and he that believes on Him shall not be confounded" (1 Pet. 2:6). Christ is the elect corner stone in Zion. The man Christ Jesus is as truly an object of election as any other man. He verily was foreordained before the foundation of the world (1 Pet. 1:20). Only He is the head of the elect world which is a glory not to be affirmed of any other. When God from eternity resolved to choose some to be the subjects of His grace and glory forever, the man Christ Jesus was first in His view, and others as members belonging to that head. Therefore, the apostle says, "God has chosen us in Him before the foundation of the world" (Eph. 1:4). The meaning of which is not that Christ is the meritorious cause of election; for indeed there was no cause of that but the mere grace and pleasure of the infinite majesty, who saw good to single out some to become his favorites. But when we are said to be chosen in Christ, it implies that Christ is the head of the elect. He is not in time, but in order of nature the first elect; though not the cause of election. Hence, He was able to speak as in John 17:6, "I have manifested Your name to the men you gave me out of the world; yours they were and you gave them me." Hence Christ does become a head not only by way of eminency, but of real union to all elect called ones. All true believers are actually united to Him, as members of the body are to the head. Now this is a most wonderful glory. To this sense some interpret that Scripture: "and gave him the head over all things to the Church" (Eph. 1:22); the words may be read thus, *and gave Him above all to be head to the Church*: as if the apostle should say, God has given Christ to be above principalities and powers, but above all the rest, there is this dignity conferred upon him, that he is made head of the Church. However, it is a truth that this is a far greater glory than to be ruler of the whole world besides.

**The man Christ Jesus sits at the right hand of God**
It was by the spirit of prophesy foretold so that it should be, long before the Son of God became a man. David spoke of Christ, when he said, "The Lord said to my Lord, sit you at my right hand" (Ps. 110:1). And the two last verses in the 16$^{th}$ Psalm are meant not of David, but of Christ: "You will not leave my soul in hell, neither will you suffer your holy one to see corruption, You will show me the path of life: in your presence is fullness of joy, at your right hand there are pleasures forever more." Says Christ, though I shall be laid in the grave; I shall not continue there so long as to see corruption, but God will make me alive again, and bring me into His presence in heaven, there to enjoy everlasting pleasures at His own right hand.

And the gospel gives us clear information concerning the accomplishment hereof; and when it was that the human nature of Christ was thus glorified, namely, "after He had suffered for the sins of His people. This man after He had offered one sacrifice for sins, forever sat down at the right hand of God" (Heb. 10:12). And in Hebrews 1:3, "when He had by Himself purged our sins, He sat down on the right hand of Majesty on high. The high priest after he had offered a solemn anniversary sacrifice, went into the holy place but did not sit down there; whereas the man Christ Jesus (the great high priest of our Christian profession) after He had offered Himself a sacrifice for sin, went to heaven and is there sat down at the right hand of Majesty that is of God, whom the Hebrews are wont to call by the name of *Majesty*.

Now when it is said that Christ "sits at the right hand of God," we are not to think (as ignorant people do) that this is to be understood literally, or as if the expression were a proper form of speech: for God is a spirit, and has not a right hand and a left, as men have. Nor may we suppose that the man Christ Jesus is always sitting now that He is in heaven. Hence sometimes in the Scripture He is represented as standing at the right hand of God. "Stephen being full of the Holy Ghost, looking up steadfastly into heaven saw the glory of God, and Jesus standing at the right hand of God" (Acts 7:55). Nor are we to believe that the man Christ does always abide just in the same place, but that He moves to and fro commanding over the host of heaven as pleases Him.

But when it is said that the man Jesus sits at the right hand of God, the meaning of that expression is that that man is next to God in glory. Heavenly mysteries are in the Scripture expressed by earthly similitudes, that we may be able to conceive something of them. Amongst men when a king sits on his throne, the man that sits on his right hand is in dignity next to him, he's the second in the kingdom; thus there is none in heaven above the man Christ Jesus except only God the Father. As the king of Egypt said to Joseph (the true type of Christ) "You shall be over my house, and according to your word shall all my people be ruled, only in the throne will I be greater than you" (Gen. 41:40). After the like manner does God speak to the man Christ Jesus saying, "my whole family in heaven and on earth shall be ruled according to your word, only in the throne will I be greater than you." In this respect the man Christ Jesus is more glorious than any of the children of men;

yes, than all the angels in heaven. "Unto which of the angels said he at any time, sit you at my right hand until I make thine enemies your foot stool" (Heb. 1:13). This session at the right hand of God, is the highest degree of glorious exaltation. The first degree of Christ's exaltation was in His resurrection from the dead; this is common to all believers, with and for the sake of Christ their head. The second degree of Christ's exaltation was in His ascension to heaven; this also may be affirmed of all the elect after the Day of Judgment.

But it cannot be said of any man except Christ alone, that He ever did or ever shall "sit at the right hand of God." To sit at His right hand is to be installed into the very throne of God. Hence is that expression, "Jesus is sat down at the right hand of the throne of God" (Heb. 12:2), which shows that Christ's being at the right hand of God, implies His being set down on the same throne which God is said to sit upon. This is peculiar to the man Christ Jesus. Glorified saints sit upon Christ's throne, but only Christ sits upon God's throne (Rev. 3:21). When the Lord Jesus ascended into heaven, God did (to speak after the manner of men) set a crown upon his head. "We see Jesus who was made a little lower than the angels, for the suffering of death, crowned with glory and honor" (Heb. 2:9). Now that which the Spirit of God helps us to believe, that which we see by faith; holy angels and glorified saints which were then in heaven, saw really done and acted before their eyes, after a blessed and heavenly manner. They saw that very Jesus who was once a babe lying in a manger on the earth, that Jesus who was once, bleeding and dying on the cross, that Jesus they saw crowned with glory and honor in the highest heaven: and they heard the word come out of the mouth of the most high God, requiring all the host of heaven to worship that very

## The Human Nature of Christ

Jesus, "let all the angels of God worship him" (Heb. 1:6). Christ the king of glory was no sooner got within the everlasting gates of heaven, but God set him at his own right hand, saying, "Here is my Son; all you glorified saints and angels adore Him." "Here is my Son (says the eternal God) come to heaven, behold all you angels of mine, I set Him above you all, and see that you worship Him."

### The blessed body of Christ now in heaven shines with unconceivable glory

There was a glimpse of this appearing at the time when Christ was transfigured before three of His disciples, "and His face did shine as the sun, and His rayment was white as the light" (Matt. 17:2). Unto that glorious transfiguration the apostle John (no doubt) has respect when he says, "we beheld His glory, the glory as of the only begotten Son of the Father" (John 1:14). For at the same time God said from heaven, "this is my beloved Son" (Matt. 3:17). The bodies of saints shall have a marvelous luster upon them after the resurrection (1 Cor. 15:43— "It is raised in glory").

But the body of Christ is far more glorious than theirs shall be: For indeed it is the exemplar which the bodies of glorified saints shall only hold some proportion with. "The Lord Jesus Christ shall change our vile body, that it might be fashioned like unto His glorious body" (Phil. 3:21). There is one glory of the sun, and another glory of the stars (as the Scripture speaks). Such a difference there is and will be to eternity, between the glory of the human nature of Jesus Christ and what believers shall in the world to come attain unto. Their glory will fall short of Christ's, as much as that of the stars comes short of the light and glory of the sun. The blessed body belonging to the Son of

God, is now brighter than ten thousand suns would be. Hence when Christ appeared to Paul as he was in the way to Damascus, though it was mid-day, "he saw a light from heaven, above the light of the Sun, shining round about him" (Acts 26:13). That body now fills the third heaven with glory. And shall at the Day of Judgment fill all this visible world with glory. It is said of the New Jerusalem, that "it has no need of the sun neither of the moon to shine in it, for the glory of God does lighten it, and the Lamb is the Light thereof" (Rev. 21:23). When the souls which are now in heaven shall come down from thence with Jesus Christ, and be reunited to their bodies, and continue in this lower world as long as the Day of Judgment shall last, then does New Jerusalem come down from God out of heaven. There will be no need of the sun to enlighten that world, the Lamb even the man Christ Jesus will be the sun, the light thereof. Well then might the inspired Psalmist say, "He is fairer then the children of men" (Ps. 45:2). But whence is all this?

I shall mention but one reason of it, which indeed is the true and great reason of all those glorious royalties belonging to this man who is fairer than the children of men.

Reason: *It is because the human nature of Jesus Christ is personally united to the eternal Son of God.* The angel Gabriel said to the mother of Christ, "that holy thing which shall be born of you, shall be called the Son of God" (Luke 1:35). The man Jesus is personally one with Him "who is over all God blessed forever" (Rom. 9:5). So that whoever looks upon Jesus Christ must say that man there is God. The fullness of the Godhead dwells in Him bodily, that is personally (Col. 2:9). And thence the man Jesus when he conversed among mortals in this lower world, He was wont to speak like a God. He did ordinarily express Himself after such a manner as never man did the like. Speaking of God He said, "My Father works hitherto, and I work" (John 5:17). Did God make the world? So did I, said Christ. Does God preserve the world? So do I. Does God quicken whom He will? So do I, says Jesus. When the Jews heard Him that was a man talking after such a rate, they thought He was the greatest blasphemer that ever breathed. And the truth is, that if any other man that ever lived on the earth, should have expressed himself as the man Christ Jesus was wont to do, he would have been guilty of the highest blasphemy. But because the man is God as well as man, all that he spoke was true, and could only be true; because of His being one in person with God. It was no more possible for that man to speak untruth, than for God to lie. If the man Jesus had sinned, it might have been said God has sinned, which to imagine is high blasphemy. A man's soul is not more truly united to his body, than the Godhead is united to the human nature of Jesus Christ: which is more than can be said of any creature excepting only the singular human nature of Christ. Now by virtue of the hypostatical union, that man becomes the Son of God. And because He is the Son of God, all the glory that possibly can be, becomes His due. That indeed, when the man Christ Jesus ascended into heaven and there sat down at the right hand of God, He did but take His place according to the dignity of His person. And because of this it is but necessary that all the angels in heaven should be made subject to that man. Yes, and that all creatures in the whole world should be put under His feet.

*Use. Let it affect all our hearts, to consider of the glory of Christ.*
Something by way of motive, and by way of counsel: Let me briefly speak to you.

Consideration 1. *It is not possible for any of us to set our hearts upon a more glorious object than Christ is.* The most glorious persons and things that ever have been in the world, were only types of Him, and did but show a faint resemblance of His glory. Was not Joseph a glorious person when he said to his brethren, "you shall tell my father of all my glory" (Gen. 45:13). He was but a type of Christ. When the high priest appeared with glorious holy garments upon him, how glorious was he! Yet he was but a type of Christ. Behold King Solomon upon his throne, the most excellent person in the whole world, and only a type of Christ. As the Lord speaks concerning the lilly, "Solomon in all his glory was not arrayed like one of these" (Matt. 6:29). So I say, Solomon in all his glory was not arrayed like this Man: He was not arrayed with MAJESTY and bedecked with GLORY as the man Christ Jesus is. His human nature is now so glorious as that no mortal eye is able to look upon it. The apostle John, while Christ was in His state of humiliation, lay in His bosom; being admitted into the greatest familiarities of love. Yet this apostle when he had a miraculous sight of Christ in glory, he says, "when I saw Him, I fell down at His feet as dead" (Rev. 1:17). If Christ as He is now in glory, should appear to any of us, we should fall down dead before Him. But what then is the glory of Christ considered as GOD! So He is the Lord of glory. What a glorious person is Jesus Christ, in whom created glory in the highest degree, and uncreated GLORY meet together! All the angels in heaven are amazed at His glory. The seraphims when they behold His glory cover their faces as acknowledging their unworthiness and their inability to look upon that glory: "and one cried unto another and said, Holy, Holy, Holy, is the Lord of Hosts, the whole earth is full of his glory" (Is. 6:2-3). So there are thousands of angels and ten thousand times ten thousand of those ministering spirits, who are all saying to Christ, "Oh you Holy, Holy, Holy Son of God, the whole heaven is full of your glory."

Consideration 2. *It is the property of a true believer to be much affected with the glory of Christ.* The spouse in the Canticles[60] says, "My beloved (i.e. Christ) is the chief of ten thousand." When some said, "What is your beloved, more than another beloved?" The reply is, "He is altogether lovely" (Song. 5:10, 16). As for unbelievers, they never had real visions of the glory of Christ. The very language of their hearts is, "He has no form nor comeliness, and when we see him, there is no beauty that we should desire Him" (Is. 53:2). But believers (who know best) are of another mind. God has opened their eyes to see that beauty in the person of Christ that their souls are enamored with Him: "To you that believe He is precious" (1 Pet. 2:7). This is the chief reason why believers are willing to die and to leave this world, it is because they would gladly see the glory of Christ. "I desire to depart and to be with Christ" (Phil. 1:23). Ay, that is the reason why they are willing to depart out of the world. It is so that they might be with Christ and have a blessed sight of His glory.

Consideration 3. *Glorified saints are affected with nothing more than this.* They think themselves most happy in that they have a sight of Christ's glory. Wherefore Christ in His last

---

[60] Song of Solomon.

prayer said, "Father, I will that they also whom you have given me, be with me where I am, that they may behold my glory which you have given me" (John 17:24). That is the heaven of heaven itself, even to behold the glory of Christ. Saints in heaven see Him face to face: "they shall see His face" (Rev. 22:4). Yes, they shall see Him "as He is" (John 3:2). Dying Stephen saw Jesus at the right hand of God. So a believer is no sooner dead than he has a soul ravishing sigh of the man Christ Jesus at the right hand of God. The saints in heaven have an intellectual vision of the glory of Christ, such as the holy angels have, and after the resurrection shall behold Christ with bodily eyes. Hence Job said, "in my flesh I shall see God" (Job 19:26-27). That is the principle reason why bodily sight shall be restored to believers at the resurrection of their bodies; even so that they may with their eyes behold the glory of Jesus Christ. With those very eyes which have beheld the tokens and signs of His body, in that ordinance of the Lord's Supper, they shall look upon Him in all His glory forever. And their souls will be satisfied with that blessed sight. As Jacob said, "It is enough, Joseph my son is yet alive, I will go and see him before I die" (Gen. 45:28), so the believer when he comes to heaven, says, now I have enough: I see the glory of Jesus Christ, and now I have enough. That blessed Glory is a soul satisfying object. Hence David said, "When I awake (i.e. at the resurrection), I shall be satisfied with your likeness" (i.e. with beholding the glory of Christ); for He alone is the likeness of God (Ps. 17:15). And yet glorified saints will never be weary with looking upon the glory of Christ in heaven.

By way of counsel:

1. *Think often upon Christ and His glory.* The more a man thinks of it, the more will he be affected with it. Occasional thoughts of this should very often come into our hearts. If a Christian have at any time lived many hours in a day and had no thoughts in his heart, concerning Christ and His glory, he has cause to be humbled. But besides that, it is good and exceedingly profitable to set time apart, solemnly to meditate on the glory of Christ. A Christian shall find by experience that such meditations will wonderfully take his heart off from things here below. What is all the world when a man by faith looks upon the glory of Christ, in comparison of whom, ten thousand worlds are all as nothing. What are riches? What are honors? What are friends? What are relations? One view of the glory of Christ drowns them all, and makes them to vanish into nothing.

And such meditations tend to make the heart more holy. "Beholding the glory of the Lord we are changed into the same image, from glory to glory" (2 Cor. 3:18). He that uses himself to such meditations will certainly be a very holy man. Remember the apostle's exhortation, "Grow in grace and in the knowledge of our Lord and Savior Jesus Christ" (2 Peter 3:18). He that grows in the knowledge of Christ, will grow in grace.

2. *Prize those things which reveal the glory of Christ.* If we are duly affected with His glory, we shall do so. The gospel and the ordinances of it reveals Christ. "We behold as in a glass the glory of the Lord" (2 Cor. 3:18). The gospel is a perspective glass, and if we have an eye of faith we shall see the glory of Christ therein. And in a special manner in that blessed ordinance of the Lord's Supper— there we see His glorious love. That the eternal Son of God should become a man, and in our nature make Himself a sacrifice to divine justice, suffering in

His body and in His soul the pains of the first and of the second death, so that He might redeem us from eternal death; what glorious love was this! Here is a Song of Loves indeed. Let us sing this new song both now, and in heaven forever.

3. *Go to God for His Spirit.* There is much of the Spirit of God in those truths which concern the glory of Christ. It is the Holy Spirit that does reveal them. It is the Holy Spirit that does affect the heart with them. Hence Christ said, as in John 16:14, "The Spirit of truth shall glorify me, for He shall receive of mine, and shall show it unto you." And if the Holy Spirit make a saving revelation of Christ's glory to our souls now through faith, it will not be long before we shall see Him as He is, and forever behold His glory. In the meantime, let every true believer to his everlasting comfort remember that Scripture with which I shall conclude: "Your eyes shall see the KING in His beauty" (Is. 33:17). Amen!

*Even so come LORD JESUS!*

# Scripture Index

Genesis
  1:1 ............... 26
  1:26 ............. 10
  2:17 ............ 117
  3:15 ............. 62
  8:21 ............ 123
  16:10 ............ 48
  18:25 ........... 118
  18:16–17 ......... 48
  22:15–16 ......... 51
  24:14 ........... 112
  29:3 ............. 36
  31:11 ............ 46
  31:13 ............ 46
  41:40 ........... 143
  45:4 ............. 69
  45:13 ........... 148
  45:28 ........... 150
  48:15–16 ......... 47
Exodus
  3:14 ............. 48
  23:21 ............ 53
  23:20–21 ......... 24
  24:2 ............. 98
  30:30 ............ 92
Leviticus
  7:7 .............. 97
  16:17 ............ 98
Numbers
  12:8 ............ 137
  14:33 ........... 124
  35:31–32 ........ 125
Deuteronomy

  5:5 .............. 98
  10:17 ............ 47
  18:19 ............ 95
Joshua
  5:14 ............. 50
1 Samuel
  2:2 ............. 113
  2:25 ............ 113
  26:19 ........... 123
2 Samuel
  7:21 ............. 59
  18:33 ........... 124
  24:25 ........... 123
1 Kings
  1:48 ............ 139
  4:29 ............ 135
  8:39 ............. 50
  19:18 ............ 51
Nehemiah
  9:6 .............. 52
Job
  9:32 ............. 98
  11:6–8 ........... 34
  19:26–27 .... 47, 150
  31:27 ............ 51
  37:16 ............ 34
  38:7 ............. 24
  40:9 ............. 32
Psalms
  2:6 .............. 96
  2:7 .......... 25, 82
  2:12 ............. 51
  5:4 ............. 119

8:4 .............................. 82
8:5 .............................. 84
11:6–7 ......................... 118
16:2 .............................. 14
16:45 ............................ 14
17:15 ...........................150
22:16 ............................ 62
24:10 ............................ 48
25:6 ...............................19
29:7 .............................. 32
29:4–5 .......................... 32
45:2 ...............91, 132, 146
56:4 .............................. 60
72:17 ............................ 25
72:18 ............................ 53
83:18 .......................47, 48
89:6 .............................. 24
89:27 ..........................134
110:1 ................... 102, 142
113:5–6 ........................ 81
139:6 ........................... 35

Proverbs
2:3 ............................... 36
2:4 ............................... 36
2:5 ............................... 36
8:23 .......................49, 70
8:30 .............................. 26
8:31 .............................. 70
8:22–26 ........................ 26
8:6–7 ............................ 41
18:14 ..........................107
30:4 .............................. 22

Ecclesiastes
2:13 .............................. 33

Song of Solomon
5:16 .............................. 41

*MYSTERY OF CHRIST*

Isaiah
6:2–3 ..........................149
9:6 ...............47, 82, 90, 103
11:1–3 .......................... 92
33:15 ..........................119
33:17 ..........................152
42:1 .......................12, 116
42:6 .............................. 92
44:24 ............................ 52
47:4 .............................. 47
49:6 .............................103
49:5–6 ..........................13
50:5 .............................. 14
52:13 ............................ 14
53:1 .............................138
53:2 .............................149
53:7 .............................. 94
53:8 .............................. 23
53:10 ...................7, 62, 101
53:11 ................... 100, 124
55:3 .............................129
57:15 ............................ 49
59:2 .............................. 89
61:1 .............................115

Jeremiah
2:22 .............................128
3:23 .............................107
17:1 .............................128
31:34 ............................ 35

Lamentations
5:7 .............................124

Ezekiel
1:26 .............................139
18:20 ..........................127
18:26 ..........................124

Daniel

3:25 ............................ 22
Hosea
 4:6 ............................ 35
 12:4 ........................... 51
Micah
 5:2 ........................ 26, 49
 5:4 ............................ 14
 6:6 ........................... 128
 6:7 ............................ 80
 7:18 ........................... 53
Habakkuk
 1:13 .......................... 119

Matthew
 1:1 ............................ 61
 1:18 ....................... 22, 73
 2:2 ........................... 139
 2:11 ........................... 50
 3:11 ........................... 53
 3:15 ............... 15, 115, 126
 3:17 ... 30, 41, 115, 129, 145
 4:2 ............................ 64
 4:3 ............................ 38
 4:10 ........................... 50
 5:17 ........................... 15
 5:45 ........................... 24
 6:29 .......................... 148
 8:21 ........................... 10
 8:3 ............................ 54
 8:29 ........................... 40
 9:6 ............................ 53
 9:33 ........................... 53
 10:15 ........................ 108
 11:11 .......................... 35
 11:27 ........................ 139
 14:33 .......................... 51

Zephaniah
 3:17 .......................... 109
Zechariah
 2:8 ............................ 56
 3:8 ............................ 91
 4:11-12 ...................... 136
 6:1 ........................... 117
 12:10 .......................... 48
 13:7 ................. 10, 54, 84
Malachi
 3:1 ........................ 91, 93
 4:2 ........................... 136

 16:13 ...................... 22, 61
 16:16 .......................... 32
 16:18 .......................... 37
 16:16-17 ...................... 34
 17:2 .......................... 145
 18:20 ..................... 50, 78
 21:37 .......................... 42
 24:21 .......................... 86
 24:31 .......................... 52
 26:26 .......................... 62
 26:38 .......................... 62
 27:45 .......................... 31
 27:54 .......................... 31
 27:42-43 ...................... 30
 27:51-52 ...................... 31
 28:18 ................... 96, 139
 28:20 .......................... 79
Mark
 2:7 ............................ 53
 13:42 .......................... 77
Luke
 1:35 ........... 30, 73, 83, 146
 1:43 ........................... 83

155

| | |
|---|---|
| 2:46 | 63 |
| 2:52 | 63, 77 |
| 2:10–14 | 112 |
| 2:30–31 | 73 |
| 4:15–16 | 63 |
| 6:35 | 24 |
| 7:28 | 35 |
| 8:28 | 29 |
| 22:18 | 63 |
| 22:42 | 63, 77 |
| 22:15–16 | 63 |
| 23:46 | 63 |
| 23:39–40 | 62 |
| 24:19 | 95 |

John

| | |
|---|---|
| 1:1 | 26, 77 |
| 1:3 | 25, 52, 84 |
| 1:10 | 25 |
| 1:12 | 24 |
| 1:1422, 24, 59, 92, 136, 145 | |
| 1:15 | 49 |
| 1:16 | 136 |
| 1:18 | 56, 137 |
| 1:29 | 123 |
| 1:34 | 30 |
| 1:49 | 30 |
| 2:19 | 31, 65 |
| 2:25 | 50 |
| 3:2 | 150 |
| 3:13 | 50 |
| 3:17 | 22, 23 |
| 3:18 | 106 |
| 3:31 | 48 |
| 3:34 | 92, 134 |
| 3:35 | 139 |
| 3:36 | 44, 107 |
| 5:17 | 53, 147 |
| 5:18 | 22, 24, 84, 138 |
| 5:21 | 54 |
| 5:22 | 139 |
| 5:23 | 57 |
| 5:25 | 32 |
| 5:27 | 96 |
| 5:39 | 36 |
| 5:22–23 | 42 |
| 6:27 | 92 |
| 6:40 | 54 |
| 6:51 | 76 |
| 6:62 | 49 |
| 6:63 | 32 |
| 6:69 | 30 |
| 7:38 | 136 |
| 8:12 | 136 |
| 8:16 | 28 |
| 8:18 | 28 |
| 8:40 | 61 |
| 8:58 | 48, 49 |
| 8:6–8 | 63 |
| 10:10 | 128 |
| 10:14 | 14 |
| 10:18 | 16, 101 |
| 10:28 | 14, 22 |
| 10:30 | 28 |
| 10:31 | 93 |
| 10:35 | 47 |
| 10:36 | 30 |
| 10:29–30 | 93 |
| 11:25 | 54 |
| 11:42 | 99 |
| 12:27 | 16 |
| 13:1 | 70 |
| 14:1 | 51, 104 |

| | | | |
|---|---|---|---|
| 14:6 | 95 | 10:38 | 63, 134 |
| 14:28 | 55 | 13:2 | 92 |
| 14:31 | 93 | 17:31 | 84, 85 |
| 15:22 | 108 | 20:28 | 76 |
| 16:7 | 53 | 26:13 | 146 |
| 16:10 | 125 | 28:4 | 120 |
| 16:13 | 36 | | |

Romans

| | |
|---|---|
| 16:14 | 53, 152 |
| 16:27 | 71 |
| 17:1 | 62 |
| 17:3 | 35 |
| 17:4 | 93 |
| 17:5 | 49 |
| 17:6 | 19, 141 |
| 17:9 | 101 |
| 17:10 | 19 |
| 17:19 | 93 |
| 17:20 | 101 |
| 17:24 | 150 |
| 17:4–5) | 16 |
| 18:9 | 100 |
| 20:17 | 14 |
| 20:31 | 43 |
| 21:17 | 50, 77 |

Acts

| | |
|---|---|
| 2:24 | 109 |
| 2:38 | 51 |
| 3:12 | 54 |
| 3:16 | 54 |
| 3:23 | 41 |
| 7:26 | 90 |
| 7:55 | 143 |
| 7:59 | 51, 57 |
| 8:37 | 40 |
| 9:20 | 37 |
| 9:21 | 51 |

| | |
|---|---|
| 1:4 | 31 |
| 1:25 | 52 |
| 1:32 | 119 |
| 2:15 | 120 |
| 3:7 | 89 |
| 3:25 | 129 |
| 3:23–25 | 126 |
| 3:25–26 | 18 |
| 3:5–6 | 118 |
| 5:1 | 122 |
| 5:10 | 122 |
| 5:11 | 122 |
| 5:19 | 100, 128 |
| 5:10–11 | 97 |
| 5:6–7 | 124 |
| 8:3 | 15, 24 |
| 8:4 | 63 |
| 8:32 | 76, 121 |
| 8:34 | 76, 105 |
| 9:4 | 45 |
| 9:5 | 85, 146 |
| 10:10 | 40 |
| 11:33 | 34 |
| 15:8 | 55 |
| 15:12 | 51 |

1 Corinthians

| | |
|---|---|
| 1:2 | 51 |
| 1:24 | 28, 138 |
| 2:8 | 48 |

| | |
|---|---|
| 2:10 | 56 |
| 2:16 | 56 |
| 5:7 | 123 |
| 6:15 | 85 |
| 6:18 | 85 |
| 6:20 | 110, 123 |
| 7:23 | 123 |
| 11:24 | 84 |
| 11:27 | 86 |
| 15:3 | 124 |
| 15:22 | 100 |
| 15:45 | 62 |
| 15:43— | 145 |
| 16:22 | 42 |

2 Corinthians

| | |
|---|---|
| 3:18 | 151 |
| 4:6 | 137 |
| 5:17 | 20, 108 |
| 5:19 | 122 |
| 5:14-15 | 124 |
| 6:15 | 108 |
| 9:18-19 | 90 |
| 13:5 | 106 |

Galatians

| | |
|---|---|
| 1:1 | 92 |
| 1:15 | 33 |
| 2:20 | 44 |
| 2:21 | 101 |
| 3:10 | 117 |
| 3:13 | 15, 99, 124 |
| 3:19 | 98 |
| 3:20 | 11, 89 |
| 4:4 | 15, 61, 77, 82, 94 |
| 4:5 | 24 |
| 5:2 | 129 |
| 5:24 | 108 |

| | |
|---|---|
| 6:14 | 20 |

Ephesians

| | |
|---|---|
| 1:3 | 70 |
| 1:4 | 141 |
| 1:14 | 110 |
| 1:17 | 14 |
| 1:22 | 141 |
| 2:3 | 89 |
| 2:14 | 90 |
| 3:4 | 34, 78 |
| 3:12 | 69 |
| 3:9-10 | 18 |
| 4:13 | 36 |
| 5:1 | 24 |
| 5:30-32 | 79 |

Philippians

| | |
|---|---|
| 1:18 | 95 |
| 1:19 | 53 |
| 1:23 | 149 |
| 2:6 | 24, 28, 84 |
| 2:7 | 126 |
| 2:9 | 31 |
| 2:10 | 43 |
| 2:9-11 | 14 |
| 3:8 | 5, 33 |
| 3:21 | 64, 145 |

Colossians

| | |
|---|---|
| 1:15 | 27, 134, 137 |
| 1:17 | 49, 53 |
| 1:18 | 134 |
| 1:19 | 134 |
| 1:20 | 122 |
| 2:2 | 5 |
| 2:3 | 135 |
| 2:9 | 72, 146 |
| 2:14 | 95, 128 |

1 Thessalonians
  1:16 ............................107
2 Thessalonians
  1:6 .............................118
1 Timothy
  2:1 .............................105
  2:5 ....... 61, 67, 75, 98, 105
  2:6 .............................123
  3:16 .............60, 62, 72, 79
  4:1 .............................105
2 Timothy
  1:9 ............................... 18
  2:13 ............................121
Titus
  2:13 ............................. 47
Hebrews
  1:1 ............................... 96
  1:2 .............................139
  1:3 27, 28, 53, 124, 142
  1:5 .......................... 23, 31
  1:6 ......................... 43, 145
  1:8 ............................... 78
  1:12 ............................. 78
  1:13 ............................144
  2:9 ..............................144
  2:11 ........................ 67, 68
  2:14 ............................. 74
  2:16 ............................. 74
  2:17 ............................. 81
  2:9–10 ....................... 100
  3:1 ...............................91
  3:3 ..............................137
  4:14 ............................. 96
  4:15 ........................ 63, 81
  4:16 ............................112
  5:2 ............................... 81

5:4 ............................... 92
5:7 ............................... 64
5:12 ............................. 32
6:18 ............................121
7:3 ............................... 49
7:22 ................94, 99, 124
7:25 ...............109, 110, 128
7:28 ...................... 93, 102
8:1 ................................91
8:2 ............................... 65
8:6 ................................91
9:7 ............................... 98
9:11 ............................. 65
9:14 ............................. 56
9:15 ............... 13, 102, 123
9:24 .............................105
9:27 ............................. 117
9:28 .............................123
10:4 ....................... 97, 123
10:5 ........................ 67, 73
10:7 ............................. 67
10:10 ............... 13, 62, 123
10:12 ...........................142
10:20 ............................ 66
10:22 ...........................124
11:11 ........................... 102
11:40 ..................... 17, 102
12:2 .............................144
12:23 ...........................134
12:24 ..............87, 103, 111
13:8 .............................. 76
13:10 ...........................123
James
  1:1 ...............................51
  2:19 ............................. 40
1 Peter

| | |
|---|---|
| 1:12 | 79 |
| 1:20 | 141 |
| 1:21 | 56 |
| 1:10–11 | 33 |
| 2:6 | 141 |
| 2:7 | 149 |
| 2:24 | 62, 124 |
| 3:18 | 6 |
| 3:19 | 56 |
| 3:22 | 140 |

2 Peter

| | |
|---|---|
| 1:10 | 106 |
| 1:16–18 | 30 |
| 3:18 | 151 |

1 John

| | |
|---|---|
| 1:6 | 108 |
| 2:1 | 97 |
| 2:2 | 122 |
| 2:23 | 37 |
| 2:1–2 | 97 |
| 3:8 | 22, 80 |
| 3:10 | 24 |
| 3:16 | 76 |
| 4:15 | 41 |
| 4:17 | 113 |
| 5:7 | 28, 73 |
| 5:13 | 5 |
| 5:20 | 47 |
| 6:7 | 79 |

Revelation

| | |
|---|---|
| 1:1 | 51, 77, 96 |
| 1:5 | 124, 133 |
| 1:7 | 62 |
| 1:8 | 48 |
| 1:14 | 49 |
| 1:17 | 148 |
| 1:13–14 | 29 |
| 2:1 | 50 |
| 2:18 | 50 |
| 2:23 | 50 |
| 3:12 | 14 |
| 3:14 | 52 |
| 3:21 | 105, 139, 144 |
| 5:2 | 140 |
| 5:13 | 52 |
| 8:3 | 105 |
| 9:6 | 103 |
| 11:18 | 21 |
| 12:15 | 39 |
| 13:6 | 65 |
| 13:8 | 17, 101 |
| 15:4 | 119 |
| 19:12 | 50 |
| 19:13 | 28 |
| 19:16 | 133 |
| 21:23 | 146 |
| 22:4 | 150 |
| 22:13 | 49 |
| 22:16 | 140 |

www.ingramcontent.com/pod-product-compliance
Lightning Source LLC
Chambersburg PA
CBHW021445070526
44577CB00002B/262